Pablo Neruda

Consulting Editors

Rodolfo Cardona
professor of Spanish
and comparative literature,
Boston University

James Cockcroft
visiting professor of Latin American
and Caribbean studies,
State University of New York at Albany

Hispanics of Achievement

Pablo Neruda

Joseph Roman

Chelsea House Publishers
New York   Philadelphia

CHELSEA HOUSE PUBLISHERS

Editor-in-Chief: Remmel Nunn
Managing Editor: Karyn Gullen Browne
Copy Chief: Mark Rifkin
Picture Editor: Adrian G. Allen
Art Director: Maria Epes
Assistant Art Director: Noreen Romano
Manufacturing Director: Gerald Levine
Systems Manager: Lindsey Ottman
Production Manager: Joseph Romano
Production Coordinator: Marie Claire Cebrián

Hispanics of Achievement
Senior Editor: John W. Selfridge

Staff for PABLO NERUDA
Associate Editor: Philip Koslow
Copy Editor: Sol Liebowitz
Editorial Assistant: Danielle Janusz
Designer: Robert Yaffe
Picture Researcher: Joan Beard
Cover Illustration: Bill Donahey based on a photograph © Luis Poirot

3 5 7 9 8 6 4 2

Library of Congress Cataloging-in-Publication Data
Roman, Joseph.
    Pablo Neruda/Joseph Roman.
        p.   cm.—(Hispanics of achievement)
    Includes bibliographical references and index.
    Summary: Describes the life and times of the Chilean poet and
diplomat.
    ISBN 0-7910-1248-4
        0-7910-1275-1 (pbk.)
    1. Neruda, Pablo, 1904–73—Biography—Juvenile literature. 2.
Poets, Chilean—20th century—Biography—Juvenile literature. [1.
Neruda, Pablo, 1904–73. 2. Authors, Chilean.] I. Title. II. Series.
PQ8097.N4Z738 1992   91-18014
861—dc20   CIP
[B]   AC

Table of Contents

Hispanics of Achievement

Oscar Arias Sánchez
Costa Rican president

Joan Baez
Mexican-American folksinger

Rubén Blades
Panamanian lawyer and entertainer

Jorge Luis Borges
Argentine writer

Juan Carlos
King of Spain

Pablo Casals
Spanish cellist and conductor

Miguel de Cervantes
Spanish writer

Cesar Chavez
Mexican-American labor leader

El Cid
Spanish military leader

Roberto Clemente
Puerto Rican baseball player

Salvador Dalí
Spanish painter

Plácido Domingo
Spanish singer

Gloria Estefan
Cuban-American singer

Gabriel García Márquez
Colombian writer

Pancho Gonzales
Mexican-American tennis player

Francisco José de Goya
Spanish painter

José Martí
Cuban revolutionary and poet

Rita Moreno
Puerto Rican singer and actress

Pablo Neruda
Chilean poet and diplomat

Antonia Novello
U.S. surgeon general

Octavio Paz
Mexican poet and critic

Javier Pérez de Cuéllar
Peruvian diplomat

Pablo Picasso
Spanish artist

Anthony Quinn
Mexican-American actor

Oscar de la Renta
Dominican fashion designer

Diego Rivera
Mexican painter

Linda Ronstadt
Mexican-American singer

Antonio López de Santa Anna
Mexican general and politician

George Santayana
Spanish philosopher and poet

Junípero Serra
Spanish missionary and explorer

Lee Trevino
Mexican-American golfer

Diego Velázquez
Spanish painter

Pancho Villa
Mexican revolutionary

CHELSEA HOUSE PUBLISHERS

INTRODUCTION

Hispanics of Achievement

Rodolfo Cardona

The Spanish language and many other elements of Spanish culture are present in the United States today and have been since the country's earliest beginnings. Some of these elements have come directly from the Iberian Peninsula; others have come indirectly, by way of Mexico, the Caribbean basin, and the countries of Central and South America.

Spanish culture has influenced America in many subtle ways, and consequently many Americans remain relatively unaware of the extent of its impact. The vast majority of them recognize the influence of Spanish culture in America, but they often do not realize the great importance and long history of that influence. This is partly because Americans have tended to judge the Hispanic influence in the United States in statistical terms rather than to look closely at the ways in which individual Hispanics have profoundly affected American culture. For this reason, it is fitting that Americans obtain more than a passing acquaintance with the origins of these Spanish cultural elements and gain an understanding of how they have been woven into the fabric of American society.

It is well documented that Spanish seafarers were the first to explore and colonize many of the early territories of what is today called the United States of America. For this reason, students of geography discover Hispanic names all over the map of the United States. For instance, the Strait of Juan de Fuca was named after the Spanish explorer who first navigated the waters of the Pacific Northwest; the names of states such as Arizona (arid zone), Montana (mountain), Florida (thus named because it was reached on Easter Sunday, which in Spanish is called the feast of Pascua Florida), and California (named after a fictitious land in one of the first and probably the most popular among the Spanish novels of chivalry, *Amadis of Gaul*) are all derived from Spanish; and there are numerous mountains, rivers, canyons, towns, and cities with Spanish names throughout the United States.

Not only explorers but many other illustrious figures in Spanish history have helped define American culture. For example, the 13th-century king of Spain, Alfonso X, also known as the Learned, may be unknown to the majority of Americans, but his work on the codification of Spanish law has greatly influenced the evolution of American law, particularly in the jurisdictions of the Southwest. For this contribution a statue of him stands in the rotunda of the Capitol in Washington, D.C. Likewise, the name Diego Rivera may be unfamiliar to most Americans, but this Mexican painter influenced many American artists whose paintings, commissioned during the Great Depression and the New Deal era of the 1930s, adorn the walls of government buildings throughout the United States. In recent years the contributions of Puerto Ricans, Mexicans, Mexican Americans (Chicanos), and Cubans in American cities such as Boston, Chicago, Los Angeles,

Miami, Minneapolis, New York, and San Antonio have been enormous.

The importance of the Spanish language in this vast cultural complex cannot be overstated. Spanish, after all, is second only to English as the most widely spoken of Western languages within the United States as well as in the entire world. The popularity of the Spanish language in America has a long history.

In addition to Spanish exploration of the New World, the great Spanish literary tradition served as a vehicle for bringing the language and culture to America. Interest in Spanish literature in America began when English immigrants brought with them translations of Spanish masterpieces of the Golden Age. As early as 1683, private libraries in Philadelphia and Boston contained copies of the first picaresque novel, *Lazarillo de Tormes*, translations of Francisco de Quevedo's *Los Sueños*, and copies of the immortal epic of reality and illusion *Don Quixote*, by the great Spanish writer Miguel de Cervantes. It would not be surprising if Cotton Mather, the arch-Puritan, read *Don Quixote* in its original Spanish, if only to enrich his vocabulary in preparation for his writing *La fe del cristiano en 24 artículos de la Institución de Cristo, enviada a los españoles para que abran sus ojos* (The Christian's Faith in 24 Articles of the Institution of Christ, Sent to the Spaniards to Open Their Eyes), published in Boston in 1699.

Over the years, Spanish authors and their works have had a vast influence on American literature—from Washington Irving, John Steinbeck, and Ernest Hemingway in the novel to Henry Wadsworth Longfellow and Archibald MacLeish in poetry. Such important American writers as James Fenimore Cooper, Edgar Allan Poe, Walt Whitman, Mark Twain, and Herman Melville all owe a sizable debt to the Spanish literary tradition. Some writers, such as Willa Cather and Maxwell Anderson, who explored Spanish themes they came into contact with in the American Southwest and Mexico, were influenced less directly but no less profoundly.

Important contributions to a knowledge of Spanish culture in the United States were also made by many lesser known individuals—teachers, publishers, historians, entrepreneurs, and others—with a love for Spanish culture. One of the most significant of these contributions was made by Abiel Smith, a Harvard College graduate of the class of 1764, when he bequeathed stock worth $20,000 to Harvard for the support of a professor of French and Spanish. By 1819 this endowment had produced enough income to appoint a professor, and the philologist and humanist George Ticknor became the first holder of the Abiel Smith Chair, which was the very first endowed Chair at Harvard University. Other illustrious holders of the Smith Chair would include the poets Henry Wadsworth Longfellow and James Russell Lowell.

A highly respected teacher and scholar, Ticknor was also a collector of Spanish books, and as such he made a very special contribution to America's knowledge of Spanish culture. He was instrumental in amassing for Harvard libraries one of the first and most impressive collections of Spanish books in the United States. He also had a valuable personal collection of Spanish books and manuscripts, which he bequeathed to the Boston Public Library.

With the creation of the Abiel Smith Chair, Spanish language and literature courses became part of the curriculum at Harvard, which also went on to become the first American university to offer graduate studies in Romance languages. Other colleges and universities throughout the United States gradually followed Harvard's example, and today Spanish language and culture may be studied at most American institutions of higher learning.

No discussion of the Spanish influence in the United States, however brief, would be complete without a mention of the Spanish influence on art. Important American artists such as John Singer Sargent, James A. M. Whistler, Thomas Eakins, and Mary Cassatt all explored Spanish subjects and experimented with Spanish techniques. Virtually every serious American artist living today has studied the work of the Spanish masters as well as the great 20th-century Spanish painters Salvador Dalí, Joan Miró, and Pablo Picasso.

The most pervasive Spanish influence in America, however, has probably been in music. Compositions such as Leonard Bernstein's *West Side Story*, the Latinization of William Shakespeare's *Romeo and Juliet* set in New York's Puerto Rican quarter, and Aaron Copland's *Salon Mexico* are two obvious examples. In general, one can hear the influence of Latin rhythms—from tango to mambo, from guaracha to salsa—in virtually every form of American music.

This series of biographies, which Chelsea House has published under the general title HISPANICS OF ACHIEVEMENT, constitutes further recognition of—and a renewed effort to bring forth to the consciousness of America's young people—the contributions that Hispanic people have made not only in the United States but throughout the civilized world. The men and women who are featured in this series have attained a high level of accomplishment in their respective fields of endeavor and have made a permanent mark on American society.

The title of this series must be understood in its broadest possible sense: The term *Hispanics* is intended to include Spaniards, Spanish Americans, and individuals from many countries whose language and culture have either direct or indirect Spanish origins. The names of many of the people included in this series will be immediately familiar; others will be less recognizable. All, however, have attained recognition within their own countries, and often their fame has transcended their borders.

The series HISPANICS OF ACHIEVEMENT thus addresses the attainments and struggles of Hispanic people in the United States and seeks to tell the stories of individuals whose personal and professional lives in some way reflect the larger Hispanic experience. These stories are exemplary of what human beings can accomplish, often against daunting odds and by extraordinary personal sacrifice, where there is conviction and determination.

Fray Junípero Serra, the 18th-century Spanish Franciscan mission-ary, is one such individual. Although in very poor health, he de-voted the last 15 years of his life to the foundation of missions throughout California—then a mostly unsettled expanse of land—in an effort to bring a better life to Native Americans through the cultivation of crafts and animal husbandry. An example from recent times, the Mexican-American labor leader Cesar Chavez has battled bitter opposition and made untold personal sacrifices in his effort to help poor agricultural workers who have been exploited for decades on farms throughout the Southwest.

The talent with which each one of these men and women may have been endowed required dedication and hard work to develop and become fully realized. Many of them have enjoyed rewards for their efforts during their own lifetime, whereas others have died poor and unrecognized. For some it took a long time to achieve their goals, for others success came at an early age, and for still others the struggle continues. All of them, however, stand out as people whose lives have made a difference, whose achieve-ments we need to recognize today and should continue to honor in the future.

Pablo Neruda

Pablo Neruda speaking at a peace conference in Paris, France, during the 1940s. When he returned to Latin America in 1943 after many years abroad, Neruda dedicated his life and his poetry to the people of his native continent.

CHAPTER ONE

The Triumph of Machu Picchu

On October 31, 1943, the 39-year-old Chilean poet and diplomat Pablo Neruda began the long climb to an ancient ruin towering 10,000 feet above the Urubamba River in the Peruvian Andes. His horse followed the switchback trail up the steep, rough walls of the mountainside, making its way slowly through the dense fog toward Machu Picchu, the last surviving remnant of the great Inca empire.

Upon reaching the summit, the poet was stunned by the awesome, majestic beauty of the site. Nestled between two peaks that towered a mile above the crashing Urubamba, whose thundering waters could be heard from the ruins, the huge and intricately laid stones seemed to grow from the earth itself. The broad stairways, the temples with their large, elegant altars, and the gabled houses were all still intact except for the thatched roofs, which had decayed over the centuries. Machu Picchu appeared much as it had originally been planned—a single architectural unit, with each stone fitted perfectly in place. Most remarkable, the giant stones were held together not by any cement but only by friction, an engineering achievement never matched either in the ancient or the modern world.

In "Alturas de Macchu Picchu" (The Heights of Machu Picchu), the long poem he wrote two years later, Neruda recaptured the exhilaration and reverence he felt:

Lofty city of laddered stones,
the home at last of all that the earth
did not hide in its slumbering garments.
In you, like two parallel lines,
the cradle of lightning and of man
rocks in a wind of thorns.

Although tourists now reach Machu Picchu fairly easily via express trains and shuttle buses, in 1943 the journey was not so simple. Earlier in the day, on October 31, Neruda had left Cuzco—the ancient capital of the Incas—by rail. On the six-hour journey, the train wound its way along the gorge created by the Urubamba River, which cascades from Cuzco toward the distant Amazon jungle. Through the window, the poet could see the ancient Inca fortresses that towered hundreds of feet above him—Ollantaytambo, Huanamarca, Wiñay-Wayna—spaced about 10 miles apart along the river.

Machu Picchu, the most majestic of these citadels, was the last one to be reached. After standing empty and neglected for hundreds of years, Machu Picchu had been rediscovered in 1911, when the explorer Hiram Bingham found the overgrown ruins perched high in the forested Andes. Thirty-two years later, Neruda had to borrow a strong horse to make the arduous journey "on the ladder of the earth, through the lost jungle's tortured thicket" up to the clear peaks above.

Surrounded on three sides by the Urubamba, Machu Picchu goes almost unmentioned in early records of the region. It was

The ruins of Machu Picchu, nestled amid the Andes Mountains at an elevation of 10,000 feet. Neruda made the arduous climb to Machu Picchu, which he called the "lofty city of laddered stones," to renew his faith in the future of Latin America.

probably built by the Inca conqueror Pachacutec in the 15th century. This was at the beginning of a period of great expansion for the Incas—an expansion that extended their domain into present-day Ecuador, Bolivia, Argentina, and Chile. The growth of the Inca empire came to a halt only with the arrival of the Spanish in 1532. Although the Spanish conquistadores subdued the Incas, they never discovered the remote Machu Picchu. With the fall of the Inca civilization, which had no written or pictographic language, the songs and oral traditions of Machu Picchu were lost.

Machu Picchu may have been a fortress, a watchtower, a populated city, or perhaps a sacred ceremonial center—its function for the Incas is far from certain. To Peruvian historian José Uriel García, Machu Picchu represented the purely spiritual triumph of the Incas, in contrast to the achievements in engineering and government for which they have been justly renowned. Uriel García, a senator from Cuzco at the time, was the man who guided Neruda on his journey through Machu Picchu. For Neruda, this magical site, towering above the Americas, became the focus of his own spiritual quest—to make his poetry a timeless monument to the life and struggle of Latin America.

Neruda was in the midst of a long-awaited homecoming. He had risen well beyond his humble beginnings in southern Chile and had now become a world figure. He had lived among the artists and poets in Paris; he had served Chile as a diplomat, first in the distant Orient and then in Mexico; he had struggled against fascism during the civil war in Spain and then fought to have Spanish refugees admitted to Chile. All the while, he had been producing poetry. Ever since the publication of his *Veinte poemas de amor y una canción desesperada* (Twenty Love Poems and a Song of Despair) in 1924, Neruda had been read and admired throughout Europe and the Americas. In scaling the Andes, he was seeking both to confirm his lifelong union with the land and the people and to uncover a new source of inspiration.

Neruda's triumphant pilgrimage through Latin America had begun two months earlier, on September 1, when he left his diplo-

A Peruvian textile dating from the 5th century B.C. The Incas, who ruled Peru from the 11th to the 16th centuries, were noted for their achievements in art and architecture. Their most spectacular construction, Machu Picchu, amazes modern scholars with its perfection of design.

matic post in Mexico. On his way back to Chile, he visited Panama and Colombia, where he read his poetry to enthusiastic audiences and spoke of the need for Latin America to develop a culture distinct from European and North American influences. Arriving in the Peruvian capital of Lima in late October, Neruda felt that he had reached the center of his quest. He told a gathering of intellectuals, "For me Peru has been the womb of America, an arena encircled by high and mysterious stones." In deference to his Peruvian audience, Neruda tactfully avoided discussing the imperial nature of the Incas, who had so viciously tried to dominate his own Araucanian neighbors. The Araucanian Indians of Chile had fought bravely to halt the Incas from making inroads into their territory in the southern Andes, and they liked to boast that they were the only native people who were never conquered by the Spaniards. In Neruda's speech, praise for the natural majesty of the Araucanians was blended with reverence for the strong sacred powers—"the woven touch of garments and liturgy"—of the Incas.

When the poet reached Cuzco—the Inca capital built centuries earlier by the native Peruvians—he found himself at the heart of this mysterious Inca arena. The mayor of Cuzco and many of its prominent citizens came out to welcome him. A local newspaper, *El Sol*, printed the tribute of Kilko Warak'a, a poet who wrote in Quechuan, the native language of the Incas and their descendants:

> The very stones of Sacsahuamán
> Awoke from their centuries of sleep
> And opened their frozen breasts
> When they knew you had arrived.

The stones of Machu Picchu, with their stark verticality and supreme isolation, also welcomed the Chilean. At the culmination of his Andean pilgrimage, amid the verdant mountains shrouded in mist, Neruda found solace, as one of the verses in part II of his poem reveals:

How many times in the winter streets of a city or in
a bus or a boat or in the twilight, or in the densest
solitude, that of the festival nights, beneath the sound
of shadows and bells, in the very cave of human pleasure,
I wished to stop and search for the eternal inexhaustible
    vein
that I had once touched in a stone or in the lightning
    unleashed by a kiss.

Machu Picchu's grandeur did not cause Neruda to forget the unknown laborers who toiled to put its huge stones in place. In his poetry, he tried to speak through the "dead mouth" of Machu Picchu's builders and to connect their suffering with the continuing struggle of the Latin American masses.

In the solitude of the Andes, Neruda no longer felt oppressed by the desolate landscapes of modern cities and the weary struggles of their inhabitants. Longing to speak through the "dead mouth" of the common people, the poet praised the skill of the native Quechuan workers who had built Machu Picchu. But he was also aware that most of the Inca workers at Machu Picchu were slaves who might have suffered just as much as the urban workers of the 20th century.

By resurrecting these workers, with their "haircloth and bitter blood," in his imagination, Neruda was seeking inspiration from the history of the American continent, from the endless toil of humanity. He was growing into his new role, that of prophet and spokesman for the entire Latin American continent. It was a role that impelled him to join Chile's Communist party, to become a senator and a presidential candidate, and to find himself at times hunted like a criminal and forced into exile while continuing to produce a body of poetry that won him the Nobel Prize in 1972.

In October 1943, looking down from the heights of Machu Picchu, Neruda was on the threshold of his life's most active and dramatic phase. "Give me the struggle, the iron, the volcanoes," he declared in his poem. Many years later, in *Memoirs*, he confirmed the importance of Machu Picchu to his further development: "I felt Chilean, Peruvian, American. On those difficult heights, among those glorious, scattered ruins, I had found the principles of faith I needed to continue my poetry."

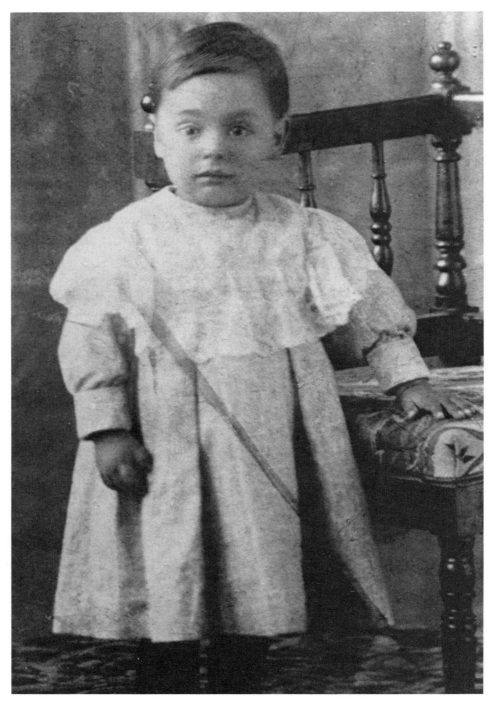

Pablo Neruda as an infant. Although he was baptized Neftalí Ricardo Reyes Basoalto, Neruda changed his name at the age of 16 to conceal his literary activities from his father, who did not want his son to be a poet.

CHAPTER TWO

Child of the Rain

My country has the shape of a great albatross with wings out-spread!" wrote Pablo Neruda in 1972. With bleak, arid deserts, rich agricultural valleys, and lush tropical rainforest, Chile's long ribbon of land extends approximately 2,600 miles from north to south. This narrow South American country—averaging only 100 miles wide—lies between the lofty mountain peaks of the Andes and the Pacific Ocean.

In the southern half of the country, where agricultural land gives way to the wet forests of the southern frontier, Neftalí Ricardo Reyes Basoalto was born in the small town of Parral on July 12, 1904. His mother, Doña Rosa Basoalto de Reyes, was a teacher in a local school for girls. Neftalí was her first and only son. Doña Rosa suffered from tuberculosis in the cold, wet winter of the Southern Hemisphere. She died a month after giving birth to Neftalí.

Neftalí's father, Don José del Carmen Reyes Morales, was a foreman on the railroad. Blond and blue eyed, he was a stern, hardworking man, used to giving orders. For two years, Don José

left Neftalí in Parral while he commanded a work train that re-
paired the tracks along Chile's railway system. After he remarried,
he brought Neftalí south to Temuco, a small frontier town. In
Temuco, Neftalí became part of a large extended family.

Neftalí's stepmother, Doña Trinidad Candia Marverde, would
provide the love and gentleness that Neftalí needed as a young
child. As was the tradition in Chile, *mamadre*, or "more-mother,"
as Neruda called his hardworking stepmother, always placed the
needs of her husband and family above her own. Feeling that her
new son was too thin, she continually fed him extra milk and bread.
In addition to caring for Neftalí, Doña Trinidad gave birth to two
children of her own in the following years—Rodolfo and Laura
Reyes Candia.

In his *Memoirs*, Neruda (a name that Neftalí would adopt in his
teens) recalled his first images of Temuco—the tall, tangled for-

*Doña Rosa Basoalto de Reyes,
Neruda's mother, died of tuberculosis a month after giving birth
to her only son. The child was
raised by his kind and loving stepmother, Doña Trinidad Candia
Marverde, whom Neruda later
called "the guardian angel of
my childhood."*

ests surrounding the town; a bird emerging from the "sunless branches" with its reedlike song; and the peasants in heavy black cloaks driving their oxen through the mud and the inexhaustible southern rain. Among the pioneer families there was a strong sense of community, with "tools and books, birthday cakes, liniments, umbrellas, tables and chairs" being freely exchanged when they were needed. In his autobiographical collection of poetry, *Memorial de Isla Negra* (Isla Negra: A Notebook), Neruda wrote of Temuco and how it affected his poetry:

> From the ax and the rain it grew
> the wooden town
> freshly cut like
> a new star with beads of resin
> and the saw and the sierra
> made love day and night
> singing
> working
> and the shrill sound of the cicada
> raising a lament
> in the stubborn solitude comes back
> as my own song.

He was also fascinated by the Araucanian Indians, who had fiercely resisted the Spanish conquerors during the 16th century. The Araucanians continued to speak their own language and held firmly to their traditional customs. Having spent his childhood on the frontier, Neruda would never lose the sense of wonder he felt while observing the Araucanians and exploring the dense, majestic forests that surrounded Temuco. He later recalled that when he traveled back and forth to the city as a student, "I always felt myself stifling as soon as I left the great forests, the timberland that drew me back like a mother. To me, the adobe houses, the cities with a past, seemed to be filled with cobwebs and silence."

Sometimes Neftalí's father would take him along on the work train. Traveling through the forests, Neftalí developed a lifelong

Years after leaving his hometown of Temuco, Chile, Neruda returned to take this photograph of a typical storefront. As a child, Neruda had been fascinated by the giant symbols—pots, boots, knives, and so on—used by shop owners to attract the many Indians and peasants who were unable to read.

love of nature. He collected partridge eggs ("blue, dark, and shiny, the color of a shotgun barrel") and beetles, some of which had shells so hard he could stand on them without crushing them. The laborers, a rugged and sometimes dangerous crew, got so caught up in the small boy's enthusiasm that they often sneaked off to hunt up specimens for him. One hulking fellow named Monge, whose face was disfigured by a knife wound, brought back a beetle that Neruda remembered as a "streak of lightning dressed in the colors of the rainbow. Red and violet and green and yellow glittered on its shell. It escaped from my hands with the speed of lightning and went back into the forest again. . . . I have never quite recovered from that dazzling apparition."

Even in Temuco, life was full of unexpected wonders. One day, while Neftalí, basically a timid child, was playing in the back of his house, a hand reached through a hole in the wooden fence and placed a small toy lamb in his hand. Neftalí quickly ran into his house and retrieved one of his favorite treasures—a pine cone—and handed it to the unknown child on the other side of the fence. He later wrote about this experience that "maybe this small and mysterious exchange of gifts remained inside me also, deep and inexhaustible, giving my poetry light."

When he was six years old, Neftalí was sent to the local school for boys, "a large rambling mansion with sparsely furnished rooms and a gloomy basement." By the time he was 10, he was already composing poems. At this time he got to know Orlando Mason, who was the editor of a journal in Temuco. Mason was the first politically aware person in Neftalí's life, vehemently defending the Araucanians against the injustices they suffered in the town. At Mason's office, Neftalí got to know the typesetters and absorbed the intoxicating smells of paper and fresh ink that rose from the printing press. The editor let the young boy blacken his hands in the thick ink, and he also published Neftalí's earliest writing in his journal.

Because many of his schoolmates mocked him for his love of poetry, Neftalí kept to himself after school, either staying at home or taking long walks in the woods. He read anything and everything he could get his hands on. He later wrote about these precious moments of solitude: "I go upstairs to my room. I read Salgari. The rain pours down like a waterfall. In less than no time, night and the rain cover the whole world. I am alone, writing poems in my math notebook."

At times Neftalí tried to hide his poetic yearnings from the other boys and reluctantly joined in their rough games. After school, he would go with them to a closed shed where they would engage in great battles, pelting each other with acorns in the dark. Neftalí usually got the worst of it. In the springtime, he and his friends would skip school as often as they could get away with it, wandering off to wade and swim in the nearby Cautín River.

At night he would struggle to stay awake and watch his father drinking and carrying on in the house until the gray light of another wet dawn trickled through the window. His father, "between his early risings and his traveling, between arriving and rushing off," tried to divert his son's attention from poetry and

*Neruda and his sister,
Laura. During family
vacations, the children
were forced to take a daily
swim in the icy waves of
the Pacific Ocean. Neruda
recalled that he and Laura
held each other's hands,
"prepared to die," until
their father allowed them
to come out.*

other literary pursuits. Sometimes he would take Neftalí to one of his favorite places, the Malleco viaduct, which stretched across the verdant mountains "like a steel violin with taut strings ready to be played by the wind of Collipulli." When these attempts failed, Don José took to punishing the boy for spending so much time alone reading, writing, and daydreaming.

In spite of his father's anger, Neftalí had his first poem published outside of Temuco when he was 14. The journal *Corre-Vuela*, located in the capital city of Santiago, accepted his poem "Mis ojos" (My Eyes), and the following year that journal accepted 13 more of his poems. His poem "Nocturno ideal" (Imaginary Night) won third prize in the Maule Floral Games poetry competition. Neftalí's early poems were steeped in nature, his blossoming desire for love, and his frustration with his education: He called his school a "sad cage" in which he wasted his childhood.

When Neftalí was 15 years old, his father was given the chance to use a friend's house in the seacoast town of Bajo Imperial. The family packed up its belongings and went off for a month's vacation. Neftalí was fascinated by Bajo Imperial, an "untamed world...

filled with horses." Watching the Araucanian riders stick like glue to their saddles even when dead drunk after a trip into town, he marveled at their ability to merge "into the wild world of nature like an animal unsure of its way but mysteriously protected." Relishing the solitude of the place and his first contact with the sea, Neftalí became accustomed to riding on horseback and would take off on long rides by himself along the deserted beach. If Neftalí's love of nature was born deep within the Andean forests, it was here, galloping along Chile's vast Pacific shores, that his love for the sea began, a love that would continue to grow throughout his life.

Bajo Imperial combined scenic beauty with the kind of mystery that was bound to inspire a young poet. On one occasion, Neftalí was invited to watch a band of workers threshing wheat up in the mountains, and soon after he set off alone on his horse. After riding for a while, he realized that he was lost and asked a peasant where he could find shelter for the night. The peasant directed Neftalí to the home of three elderly French ladies whose grandparents had come to Chile to start a lumber business. White haired and dressed in black, the three sisters maintained, in the solitude of the mountains and amid the sawdust of the lumber mill, a home that belonged to another time and place. Delighted that the young traveler was familiar with French poetry, they served him one of the best meals he had ever eaten, complete with vintage wines served in crystal glassware. In *Memoirs*, Neruda recalled:

> I went off to sleep and dropped into bed like a sack of
> onions in a market. At dawn I lit a candle, washed up and
> got dressed. It was already getting light when one of the
> stable boys saddled my horse. I didn't have the heart to say
> goodbye to the kind ladies in black. Deep in me, something
> told me it had all been a strange, magical dream, and that,
> to keep from breaking the spell, I must try not to wake up.

For many years after that first summer, the family returned to Bajo Imperial. But relations between Neftalí and his father were

A view of Puerto Aysén in southern Chile. Growing up amid the scenic beauty of his native region, Neruda developed a deep love of nature. His first books of poems were filled with images of the outdoors—the ocean, birds, wind, rain, forests, and mountains.

growing more tense. Angered that his eldest son was not pursuing a proper middle-class profession, Don José beat the boy to teach him respect for proper values. But the aspiring young poet would not be forced into a profession in which he had little or no interest. To avoid his father's anger, the adolescent adopted a pen name. Signing a poem entitled "Hombre" (Man) in his notebook, he wrote: "Pablo Neruda as of October 1920."

The young poet had chosen the name Neruda out of a magazine, not knowing much about its rightful owner, the prominent Czech writer Jan Neruda. (Many years later, when he visited Prague, Pablo Neruda placed a flower at the foot of his namesake's statue.) Neftalí's only concern was to conceal his identity from his father, and he believed that a European name would be a good disguise. His choice of Pablo (Paul) as a first name may have been inspired by his love for the poetry of the 19th-century French writer Paul

Verlaine or possibly from a later French poet, Paul Valéry. (Neruda would not legally change his name until 1946, when he was a member of the Chilean Congress.)

Back at Temuco, Neftalí felt like an outcast among the children his age. He was terribly shy around girls and was often tormented by the luring glances of two sisters who lived across the street from him. Terrible at soccer, the game that most of the other boys played after school, Neftalí would spend much of his time taking long walks through the surrounding woods and through the streets of the town.

One adult who encouraged Neftalí's literary pursuits was Gabriela Mistral, an accomplished poet who was appointed principal at the school for girls in Temuco. Mistral was an imposing figure with a "dark face, as Indian as a lovely Araucanian pitcher," and the young poet was too much in awe of her to seek her out. But when he was taken to meet her, Neftalí found her to be extremely gracious, with a "full, generous smile that lit up the room." Mistral introduced him to the works of 19th-century Russian novelists, such as Tolstoy and Dostoyevsky; the mature Neruda considered these works to be a very important influence in his literary development. Neruda never forgot Mistral's kindness and wrote a moving tribute to her in *Memoirs*.

Huddled in his home during the torrential southern rains, surrounded by books and his poetry, Neftalí began to dream of the cities and the lands beyond Temuco. When a chance to study in Santiago presented itself, he eagerly asked his father for permission. Because the course at the Instituto Pedagógico, where Neftalí would learn to teach French, seemed respectable, his father agreed to support his son in Santiago. Neftalí, eager to travel beyond the rough frontier town, began to pack his bags for the long journey north. Once he left, he would never again be known as Neftalí Ricardo Reyes Basoalto—only as Pablo Neruda.

Pablo Neruda during his student days at the University of Santiago.
Neruda promised to earn a degree in French in order to please his father,
but when he reached the capital, he spent most of his time writing poetry
and socializing with his fellow students.

CHAPTER THREE

The Santiago Twilight

In March 1921, Neruda boarded the night train to Santiago. Dressed, as always, in his black suit and carrying few possessions, the tall, thin adolescent sat in the third-class compartment of the train, which took a full day to reach the capital. He left the forests and rain of Temuco, he later wrote, with his head "filled with books, dreams, and poems buzzing around like bees."

Upon arriving in the city, the young poet was welcomed only by the noise and loneliness of the bustling streets, which he later recalled as smelling of "gas fumes and coffee." With his small monthly allowance in hand—supplied by his father with the hope that he would pursue a respectable profession—he went in search of a cheap boardinghouse. After he had settled into his room at 513 Maruri Street, he signed up to study French at the University of Santiago.

At the boardinghouse, he would watch the sun set from his window until the twilight made it too dark to see. After nightfall, Neruda had only candles to light his room. So he would take to the streets on one of his many restless night strolls around the city. He dressed in a wide sombrero and a thick gray cape that he had taken from his father, who had received it from the railroad company but had never used it. Despite his provincial background, his manner of speaking and dressing made a powerful impression on the people he met. In Santiago, Neruda played the role of the pale, starving, romantic poet to the hilt.

He recalled feeling lost during his first months in the city: "The autumn and then the winter ended with the leaves in the streets and in the parks. The world was dirtier, darker and more painful." But it was this very sense of suffering that quickly established a reputation for him in the literary circles of the capital. According to Mariano Picón-Salas, one of his friends at the time, there were

Downtown Santiago during the 1920s. Neruda enjoyed the cultural life of the city, but he was a country boy at heart. He felt himself suffocating without the lakes and forests of his native region and thought that the city smelled of "gas fumes and coffee."

students who copied Neruda's manner of dress and his restless night wanderings and who even greeted each other with quotations from Neruda's poetry.

While enjoying his popularity, Neruda was also working hard to develop his poetry. In 1921, he won first prize at the Student Federation for his poem "La canción de la fiesta" (Song of the Festival) published in the federation's journal, *Juventud* (Youth). Neruda also wrote for *Claridad* (Clarity), the student newspaper, and founded the journal *Caballo de bastos* (Jack of Clubs). The next year, Neruda had his first chance to read in front of an audience much larger than his group of student friends. He joined the Chilean poets Joaquín Cifuentes, R. Monestier, and Alberto Rojas Giménez at a joint reading in front of the esteemed Vremia literary group.

Neruda's first book, *Crepusculario* (Twilight Book), composed of poems he had written when he was 16 and 17, was published in 1923. The anarchist Juan Gandulfo provided the illustrations for the first edition. As might be expected in the work of a young poet, many of the poems were steeped in melancholy, interspersed with bold attempts at passion. The passionate side of Neruda's nature became the focus of his next book, *Veinte poemas de amor*. This collection, published the following year, was filled with long, rhythmic lines celebrating both the need for love and the difficulty of attaining it. As the lonely poet faces the "sad rage, the screaming, the solitude of the sea," he becomes lost in both the overwhelming power of nature and in his own desires.

Although at first Neruda was surprised that *Veinte poemas de amor*—written with so much agony—brought consolation to the lovers who read it, he later recognized that "in spite of its acute melancholy, the joyfulness of being alive is present in it." At the age of 20, Neruda had already established himself as a major voice in Latin American literature. The Argentine writer Julio Cortázar recalled the effect that Neruda's love poems had on other Latin American writers at the time:

He showed us that the love of a Latin American poet could
be given and written about . . . in the simple words of the
day, with the smell of our streets, with the simplicity in
which we could discover beauty without having to agree to a
grand purple style and divine proportions.

Not only were the poets listening to Neruda. The ordinary
people of Santiago and Latin America were learning his name and
poetry as well. Neruda found this out one evening when he went to
a nightclub with some friends; two local toughs got into an argu-
ment in the middle of the dance floor, and Neruda boldly told
them to stop acting like idiots and let people enjoy themselves.
When one of the men turned and stared in amazement at the
scrawny poet, the other one knocked him out with a single punch.
The dancing resumed, but the story was not over. When Neruda
left the club, he found the winner of the fight—"a kind of mountain, with the waist of a panther"—waiting for him. Refusing to
apologize for speaking up, Neruda was more or less prepared to
absorb a beating. Suddenly, the burly giant threw back his head and
asked, "Are you the poet Pablo Neruda?" When Neruda said he was,
the man almost burst into tears. He confessed that he and his
girlfriend read Neruda's poetry together all the time, until they
knew it by heart—he had no doubt that the poetry kept them
together. When Neruda's friends arrived with reinforcements, they
found the hoodlum reciting poetry. The evening ended without
bloodshed.

Neruda continued to study French. But after working on a
few translations, he decided that teaching and translating French
would not be his career, and at the age of 20, he dropped out of the
Instituto Pedagógico. His father, upset by the news, immediately cut
off his monthly allowance. Now that he had decided to become a
writer, Neruda would have to live on the little money he could earn
with his pen.

Neruda (seated at center with arms folded) poses with a group of young poets. Neruda and his friends were as interested in politics as they were in literature: They often took part in workers' demonstrations and were sometimes beaten by the police.

Many of his fellow Chileans were also struggling at this time. Demand for copper and nitrate, Chile's main exports, had been high between 1914 and 1918, when World War I raged in Europe. But when the demand dropped after the war, Chile's economy went into a tailspin. The gap between rich and poor grew wider, with the upper classes firmly in control of the government. The university students, especially Neruda's friends at the Student Federation, made it clear that they were on the side of the workers and *los rotos* (the broken ones), as Chile's oppressed army of wandering laborers was known.

In 1920, Arturo Alessandri Palma was elected president with the backing of Chile's liberals, leftists, and organized workers. Alessandri, a dynamic and fiery individual, had promised social reforms, but once in office, he found it difficult to implement his programs because the Congress was still controlled by the conservatives; the changes Alessandri did make failed to revive the ailing

economy. In 1924, the army and navy stepped in and forced Alessandri to resign. Even though Alessandri regained the presidency
the following year and finally succeeded in putting through some
of his reforms, Neruda had already lost faith in him. He threw his
support behind Luis Emilio Recabarren, a workers' leader who
later founded Chile's Communist party. Neruda wrote articles for
Claridad supporting the workers' cause and joined in street demonstrations during which he and his fellow students were beaten up by
the Santiago police. "From that time on," he recalled, "with inter-
ruptions now and then, politics became part of my poetry and my
life. In my poems I could not shut the door to the street, just as I
could not shut the door to love, life, joy, or sadness in my young
poet's heart."

*Arturo Alessandri Palma
served as president of
Chile during the early
1920s. Although Ales-
sandri attempted to put
through reforms that
would benefit the work-
ing classes, he did not go
far enough to suit the
youthful Neruda, who
was becoming more
and more radical.*

Now that he was dedicated to writing full-time, Neruda finished a new book of poetry, *Tentativa del hombre infinito* (Venture of an Infinite Man), in 1925. The poems were noticeably influenced by surrealism (a literary and artistic movement that sought to express the workings of the unconscious mind through the use of startling imagery). His book of prose sketches, *Anillos* (Rings), and a short novel, *El habitante y su esperanza* (The Inhabitant and His Hope), one of his least-read works, were also published. But he was becoming restless in Santiago, and with a friend he went to live in the village of Ancud on a remote island off the Chilean coast. However, his agitated nature was not cured by the tranquil stillness of the island, and the two young men found themselves back in Santiago within a year.

Even though his poetry was being readily accepted in Chilean journals at the time, Neruda was still poor and constantly hungry. In Santiago, he lived by moving from boardinghouse to squalid boardinghouse, forced to leave because he could not scrape up the rent money. Years later, he would write about these homeless days in his "Oda a la pobreza" (Ode to Poverty):

> When I rented a small room
> in the suburbs,
> seated on a chair,
> you were waiting for me,
> or on turning down the sheets
> in the dark hotel,
> adolescent,
> I didn't find the fragrance
> of a naked rose,
> but rather the cold hissing
> from your mouth.
> Poverty
> you followed me
> through the barracks and the hospitals,
> through peace and through war. . . .
> I saw you throw my furniture

into the streets:
the men
they let it fall like stones.

Neruda's popularity, which was growing with each volume
of poetry he published, eventually did provide him with an opportunity to escape his meager existence. Chile, like many Latin
American countries at the time, often rewarded writers with diplomatic posts in foreign countries. A friend arranged an interview for
Neruda with the head of Chile's consular service. The official spoke
to Neruda for an hour about poetry and music and sympathized
with his artistic ambitions. Finally, he shook Neruda's hand and
declared, "You may now consider yourself virtually appointed to a
post abroad."

During the next two years, while he lived from hand to mouth,
Neruda made regular visits to the friendly official, hoping to find
out when he was being sent overseas. Each time, the man greeted
him like a long-lost brother, told his secretary to hold all phone
calls, and sat down for a long talk about every subject under the
sun—except the specifics of Neruda's new job. "Although I didn't
have enough money to eat," Neruda recalled, "I would leave in the
evening breathing like a diplomat."

Finally, Neruda ran into a friend named Victor Bianchi, whose
family had powerful political connections. When Bianchi heard
that Neruda was still waiting for a job, he took him at once to see
the foreign minister. Neruda was dazzled by the speed with which
he was ushered into the foreign minister's office, though not so
dazzled that he failed to note that the minister, a very short man, sat
up on his desk to make himself look taller. When Bianchi told the
minister that Neruda was eager to go abroad, the minister immediately called in the head of the consular service. Neruda's self-styled
protector could no longer drag his feet. When the minister asked
what posts were available, he reeled off a list of names. None of the
names meant anything to Neruda, but he thought one of them had

a nice ring to it—Rangoon. That was the city Neruda chose, and just like that the order was made official.

The minister had a large globe in his office, and Neruda and Bianchi immediately went to look for Rangoon. They found it in Asia, right in the middle of a dent that someone had made in the globe. But when Neruda got together with his poet friends that night to celebrate his new job, he had completely forgotten the name of the place he was going to: "Bubbling over with joy, I could only explain that I had been named consul to the fabulous Orient and that the place I was being sent to was in a little hole in the map."

The little hole in the map was to provide countless adventures for the young poet.

*Neruda relaxes on the beach in Rangoon, Burma (present-day Myan-
mar). Neruda was lonely so far from home, and his post as Chilean
consul in Rangoon provided very little money. With only his poetry for
solace, he produced some of his finest work during this period of his life.*

CHAPTER FOUR

Residence on Earth

After a rousing send-off from their friends in Santiago, Neruda and his traveling companion, Alvaro Rafael Hinojosa, boarded a ship that was bound for the eastern coast of South America and then for Portugal. On arriving in Buenos Aires, Argentina, Neruda quickly cashed in the first-class ticket supplied to him by the Foreign Ministry. With the money he got back, he bought two third-class tickets, one for himself and one for Hinojosa, on the *Baden,* a German ship bound for Lisbon. Neruda later wrote of this voyage in his autobiographical poem "Primer viaje" (First Journey):

> For me everything was new. This planet
> was collapsing from sheer old age:
> but everything was opening so I could live it,
> so I could see that flash of lightning.

After spending a short time in Lisbon, where they devoured the fresh food they had missed during their month at sea, Neruda and Hinojosa visited Madrid and then headed for Paris. In Paris, they

A Paris sidewalk café during the 1920s. At this time, Paris was the artistic capital of the world, but Neruda found the city disappointing. During his stay, he seemed to meet only fellow Latin Americans who spent their time drinking and picking fights.

spent all their time in the artists' quarter of Montparnasse, on the Left Bank of the river Seine. To their surprise, they met no Europeans at all, only Latin Americans who seemed to spend all their time drinking cognac, dancing the tango, and looking for the chance to pick a fight with someone—the Argentines in particular were always getting tossed out of cafés by squads of waiters. Unlike many young artists of the time who felt that Paris was the center of the world, Neruda felt that the "fire had gone out" in the French capital. Before long, the two Chileans left for the Mediterranean port of Marseilles on a train that was "loaded, like a basket of exotic fruit, with a motley crowd of people, country girls, and sailors, with accordions and songs chorused by everyone in the coach."

From Marseilles, Neruda and Hinojosa finally departed for the East. While at sea, Neruda wrote endless letters to his friends back home and worked on a series of dispatches for the Santiago journal *La Nación* (The Nation). The journey was fairly uneventful until the ship put in at Shanghai, China, a seaport noted for its exotic night-life. When Neruda and Hinojosa made the rounds of the night-clubs, however, they were sorely disappointed. It was the middle of the week, and apparently most of Shanghai was getting a good night's sleep. The enormous dance halls were nearly empty, and the only company the two travelers found were some Russian women, "thin as skeletons" in Neruda's recollection, who were eager to be treated to champagne.

Thoroughly depressed, Neruda and Hinojosa headed back to their ship. Each of them hired a rickshaw, a small cart pulled by a man, and asked to be taken to the harbor. As they got under way it began to rain, and the rickshaw drivers stopped and covered the carts with cloth so their passengers could stay dry. The only trouble was that the passengers could not see where they were being taken; after what seemed like an unusually long time, the rickshaws halted, and Neruda and Hinojosa found themselves in a deserted field far from the harbor. When they got down, they were subdued by quick rabbit punches to the back of the neck. As they lay on the ground, a band of thieves quickly went through their pockets, taking all their money and much of their clothing but considerately leaving the passports and identity papers. With the help of sympathetic passersby, the two travelers made it back to their ship and continued on to Japan.

They were almost completely broke when they reached Yokohama. They found refuge in a seaman's shelter, shivering on straw mattresses laid out beneath broken windows. Their plight would have been truly desperate if not for the wreck of a tanker off the coast. The survivors were given blankets and food by the shipping company; one of them, a Spaniard, took the two Chileans under his wing and shared his provisions with them. Meanwhile, Neruda and Hinojosa went to see the Chilean consul to inquire about some money they were expecting from home. The consul showed little interest in their plight. He was sure he would be told if any money arrived and would let them know. They could not call him because he had not bothered to get a telephone; he was convinced that he would only get calls from people speaking Japanese, which he did not understand. After suffering for several more days, Neruda and Hinojosa finally got word that their money had arrived in Yokohama days before; the consul simply never took the trouble to

A view of the harbor of Shanghai, China, showing the European section of the city. On his way to Rangoon, Neruda had made an unfortunate stopover in Shanghai. Hoping to sample the nightlife, he was waylaid by thieves in a deserted area and robbed of all his money.

check. That night they went to celebrate in the best café in Tokyo, drinking toasts to "all the unfortunate travelers neglected by perverse consuls all over the world."

The gold-encrusted dome of the 2,500-year-old Shwe Dagon Pagoda welcomed Neruda to Rangoon, and the Irrawaddy River, at whose mouth the city sat, struck his poet's ear as having the most beautiful name of all the rivers in the world. But as he took up his diplomatic duties, Neruda found himself painfully isolated. Hinojosa, with whom he had shared so many adventures, had continued his wanderings, which would eventually lead him to New York. The English businesspeople and administrators who surrounded Neruda—Burma (today called Myanmar) was at the time a British colony—had little to offer the young poet in the way of intellectual stimulation. At the same time, the Burmese and the other Asians he met saw him—at least as far as he could tell—as just another agent of Western business interests. His loneliness was a constant theme in the poems he wrote at this time. In "El sur del océano" (Oceanic South), for example, he wrote:

> It is a lonely region, I have spoken
> of that so lonely region,
> where the earth is full of ocean,
> and there is no one except a few horses' hoofprints,
> there is no one but the wind, there is no one

but the rain that falls on the waters of the sea,
no one but the rain that grows above the sea.

After a year of service in Rangoon, Neruda wrote to his sister,
Laura, to express his happiness at having been transferred to
Colombo on the island of Ceylon (now called Sri Lanka). He
explained that he found his work in Burma insupportable and was
tired of living in the same place for so long. He was looking forward
to the change.

In fact, there was a more pressing reason than boredom for
Neruda's impatience to leave Rangoon. He was especially eager to
end a love affair he had begun with a Burmese woman known as
Josie Bliss. Although Neruda was fascinated by Bliss, he began to
feel that she was too possessive. According to his recollections, she
even resented the letters he received from abroad and often hid his
official telegrams. At times, he would wake up in the middle of the
night to find her circling around his bed with a knife in her hand.
"She would have ended up by killing me," he asserted. When the
time came to go to Ceylon, Neruda made his arrangements in
secret and then left without warning, leaving all his clothes and
books behind in Rangoon. He did so with a heavy heart; on the
ship that was taking him away he wrote "Tango del viudo" (The
Widower's Tango), expressing his contradictory feelings about
Bliss:

So it hurts me to think of the bright day of your legs
resting like slow, hard waters heated by the sun,
and the swallow, sleeping and flying, that lives in your eyes,
and the mad dog you shelter in your heart,
and so I also see the dead who stand between us from this
    day on,
and I breathe with the air the ashes from the ruins.
I could take this enormous sea wind to be your sudden
    breath
and the vast solitary space that surrounds me forever.

When he settled into his consular post in Colombo, Neruda once again felt lost between the colonial authorities and the "milling multitude." He rented a bungalow near the sea and resigned himself to a lonely existence. To keep him company, he adopted a dog and a pet mongoose, which he named Kiria. Together the three of them roamed the beaches near Colombo, with the dog yelping wildly whenever they came upon one of Ceylon's many elephants bathing in the sea. Neruda, always interested in animals, was amazed by the sight of these massive animals lumbering up and down the roads, carrying loads of timber. As he became more familiar with his surroundings, he had the opportunity to watch a herd of wild elephants being trapped in a huge corral and gradually tamed until they were ready to be beasts of burden.

Neruda's political awareness was heightened by a trip he made to India in 1929. In Calcutta, he attended a meeting of the Indian National Congress party, already agitating for independence from British rule. (India did not become an independent nation, however, until 1947.) While there, he met Mohandas K. Gandhi, a lawyer and the leading architect of India's nationhood.

Neruda was greatly impressed by Gandhi. A cunning politician devoted to bringing about Indian independence, Gandhi often made grand symbolic gestures in which he drew attention to the plight of the people of India under British rule. Gandhi moved the Indian masses to action by speaking, writing, and, most important, by living his own life according to his principles. That action frequently took the form of peaceful mass resistance to British colonial policies; even when British troops fired on crowds of peaceful

Mohandas K. Gandhi (1869–1948) was the architect of India's drive toward independence from British rule. During a visit to India in 1929, Neruda was deeply impressed by Gandhi.

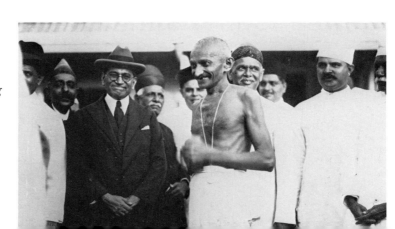

demonstrators, Gandhi insisted that his people use only nonviolent means of retaliation. Because of Gandhi's strict adherence to the principle of active nonviolent resistance, his steadfast belief in a people's God-given right to govern themselves, and his willingness to risk his life for this belief, Gandhi was revered by the Indian masses, who respectfully named him Mahatma, or Great Soul. Neruda called him "a practical man . . . a tactician . . . a saint."

In India, Neruda also met Pandit Motilal Nehru and his son Jawaharlal, who would later become India's first prime minister. In India, Neruda saw a vast population in abject poverty, with thousands dying each day of hunger and unchecked diseases. Neruda blamed the condition of the Indian people on the British colonialism that Gandhi and the Nehrus were struggling against. He greatly admired Subhas Chandra Bose, a political leader who had sided with the Japanese when they invaded India during World War I. Although Bose was tried for treason and condemned to death by a British colonial court, the British were forced to free him after widespread protests. Neruda was deeply impressed by Bose's stature as a popular hero, and echoes of Bose's influence can be seen in Neruda's later political career.

Meanwhile, Neruda was working on *Residencia en la tierra* (Residence on Earth), a book he later considered overly self-absorbed and melancholy, and he was having problems getting the book published in Santiago. Being so far from home, there was little he could do to convince Chilean publishers to accept his work.

One day, Josie Bliss showed up unexpectedly outside Neruda's house. He was afraid to let her in the door, so she camped out in his front yard. She stayed there for weeks, pouncing on anyone who tried to visit Neruda and driving them away with insults. Finally, the police told Neruda that they were going to throw Bliss out of the country unless he took her in. Somehow he convinced her to go back to Rangoon of her own accord and escorted her to the ship, where they had a dramatic and heartrending farewell scene. Looking back on this event at the age of 70, Neruda wrote that his "heart received a great scar which is still part of me." (When he returned to Burma during the 1950s, he could find no trace of Bliss; the house in which they had lived together was almost in ruins.)

In 1930, Neruda was appointed consul in both British-held Singapore and the Dutch colony of Java. His meager salary was thus doubled, and he looked forward to being raised "from the first circle of poverty into the second." While rejoicing that he would now be able to afford a bed instead of the field cot he was used to, he could not bear the thought of leaving his mongoose, Kiria. Although he realized that his behavior was more appropriate to a tycoon than to a starving consul from a small Latin American country, he decided to take his servant, Bhampy, with him to Singapore; Bhampy, a resourceful fellow, found a way to smuggle the little mongoose past the customs inspectors.

After discovering, to his dismay, that there was no Chilean consulate for him to occupy in Singapore, Neruda landed in Batavia (now Djakarta) on the island of Java. By registering the occasional shipments of goods between Chile and the Dutch East Indies and collecting a fee for his services, he made enough of a living to support himself, Bhampy, and Kiria. Though he continued to feel lonely and cut off from the world, he enjoyed the outdoor cafés and the enormous feasts of Indonesian delicacies served up in a nearby hotel. All in all, Neruda's life was fairly tolerable until he lost Kiria. The mongoose had been in the habit of following Neruda wherever he went, and one day she disappeared in the whirl of the city's traffic. Neruda placed ads in the papers and looked for Kiria everywhere, but his beloved pet was clearly gone. Bhampy, who took the loss of the mongoose as a personal disgrace, went back home to Ceylon, leaving Neruda all alone.

Neruda must have made some acquaintances in Batavia, because on December 6, 1930, he married María Antonieta Hagenaar Vogelzanz, an Indonesian of Dutch extraction. Blue eyed and taller than Neruda, Maruca (as her new husband called her) spoke no Spanish, and because he could not speak Dutch, they communicated in English. Neruda wrote to his father about his marriage, apologizing for his haste: "I wanted to tell you of my decision to marry and to wait for your consent, but due to numerous circumstances, our marriage was consummated well before the date we had planned." The railwayman's reply—if there was one—to this message from his wayward son has not been preserved.

In 1932, after 75 days at sea, Neruda and his wife returned to Chile. His homecoming, however, was not as joyous as he had hoped. Chile had been hit hard by the Great Depression, and the political conditions prevailing in the country were equally disturbing to Neruda. Carlos Ibáñez del Campo, an army colonel who had taken office in 1927 through a rigged election, was now president. Once in office, he had also manipulated the congressional elections, bringing his own legislators to power. During his four years in office, Ibáñez del Campo had governed by dictatorship, paying little attention to the democratic provisions in the Chilean constitution. Although liberal elements had attempted some economic reforms—industrial products were introduced, some of the mines were partly taken over by the government, public education was improved, and public works were spread to rural areas—a handful of powerful families still controlled Chile's government.

Neruda did have something to console him upon his return to Santiago, however. His books *El hondero entusiasta* (The Ardent Slingsman) and *Residencia en la tierra* were released during the next few months. Although most of the poems included in *Residencia en la tierra* were composed during his stay in Asia, Neruda insisted that the influence of those foreign countries was minimal on his verse. Yet the scope of this book—with its wide view of the tragic nature of the world—surely was a result of his extensive travels and his experiences with so many different cultures.

In spite of the popularity of his work, Neruda could not live on his poetry alone. After a year at the ministry in Santiago, he was appointed to a consular post in Buenos Aires. This time his wanderings would change his life and his poetry forever.

General Francisco Franco (arm outstretched) reviews his victorious troops at the end of the Spanish civil war in 1939. The war, in which Fascist forces brought down Spain's democratic government, was a turning point in Neruda's life.

CHAPTER FIVE

The Bridge of Commitment

In May 1934, after spending less than a year in Buenos Aires, Neruda was pleased to accept a transfer to Barcelona, Spain. It did not take long for Neruda's new boss, Tulio Maqueira, the consul general of Chile in Spain, to learn that Neruda was not adept at doing the nuts-and-bolts arithmetic that was the main work of the consulate. After watching Neruda struggle with columns of figures, Maqueira generously told his new assistant: "Pablo, you should go live in Madrid. That's where the poetry is. All we have here in Barcelona is that terrible multiplication and division that certainly doesn't need you around. I can handle it."

Neruda joyfully went off to Madrid and found that many of the poets in the Spanish capital had already heard of him. Neruda had struck up a friendship with Federico García Lorca, one of Spain's leading poets, during Lorca's visit to Buenos Aires in 1933. The poet Rafael Alberti, who helped Neruda get settled, had been reading poems from *Residencia en la tierra* to visitors in his home on Marqués de Urquijo Street ever since receiving the book a few months earlier. Neruda later wrote in tribute to his friends: "When you accepted me as one of you, you gave such a sense of security, such meaning to my life, and to my poetry, I went with serenity to join the struggle among the ranks of the people."

The poets who became Neruda's friends in Madrid were united in support of the Spanish Republic, which had been established in 1931. Throughout its history, Spain had been ruled by kings and queens and the Catholic church had been the most powerful social force in the nation. But with the Great Depression ravaging Spain and much of the population pushing for radical change, King Alfonso XIII stepped aside in favor of a republican government. The new government, an uneasy coalition between competing groups, was in trouble from the start. The privileged classes, with the support of the army and the Church of Spain, were determined to block reform and restore the monarchy; on the other hand, left-wing groups pushed for more drastic reforms, responding with protests and strikes when the government moved too slowly. Spain was slowly moving toward the violent confrontation that finally erupted in 1936.

As the political situation in Spain grew more tense, so did the atmosphere in Neruda's household. He and his wife, Maruca, were finding it increasingly difficult to get along, and their relationship was not helped by Neruda's paltry income and inability to pay the

Neruda (back row, fourth from right) and a group of Spanish writers and artists in Madrid. When he arrived in Spain in 1934, Neruda found that many of the leading Spanish poets knew and admired his work. He thanked them for giving him a new sense of security and political dedication.

bills. Despite the couple's conflicts, Maruca gave birth to a daughter, Malva Marina, on October 4, 1934. The birth was extremely difficult, and in the course of it Malva Marina suffered injuries that impeded her physical development. She died in Europe in 1942, at the age of eight.

As his marriage was falling apart, Neruda grew ever closer to the Argentine painter Delia del Carril, 20 years older than he, whom he met in the home of the Chilean ambassador. Del Carril was to have a great influence on Neruda's poetry and politics for the next 15 years.

In December 1934, Neruda gave a reading at the University of Madrid. Federico García Lorca introduced Neruda to the audience, praising the Chilean's "full, romantic, cruel, wild, mysterious, American" poetry. A short time after the reading, *Residencia en la tierra* was published in Madrid along with a Spanish edition of *Veinte poemas de amor*. Neruda was quickly acquiring a large and loyal readership in Spain. In February 1935, when Neruda was officially appointed consul in Madrid, replacing his old teacher Gabriela Mistral, many prominent young writers, including Lorca, Alberti, and Jorge Güillén joined together to honor his work publicly, claiming that his poetry represented "without dispute one of the most authentic realities in the Spanish language today."

The Nerudas lived in Argüelles, a neighborhood of markets filled with the shouts of merchants and the smell of seafood. With the backing of his friends, Neruda became the editor of a literary review, *Caballo verde* (Green Horse). First released in October 1935, *Caballo verde* contained the work of many of the poets Neruda knew in Madrid. Writing introductions to the first few issues, Neruda stressed the importance of everyday life in poetry. In the tradition of the American poet Walt Whitman, he argued that poetry should be all-inclusive, celebrating the world as it was, its ugliness as well as its beauty. This growing rejection of literary references and refinement would become stronger in Neruda's poetry throughout the following years.

ODA AL LIBRO (II)

Nosotros
los poetas
caminantes
exploramos
el mundo,
en cada puerta
nos recibió la vida,
participamos
en la lucha terrestre.
¿Cuál fue nuestra victoria?
Un libro,
un libro lleno
de contactos humanos,
de camisas,
un libro
sin soledad, con hombres
y herramientas,
un libro
es la victoria.
Vive y cae
como todos los frutos,
no sólo tiene luz,
no sólo tiene sombra,
se apaga,
se deshoja,
se pierde
entre las calles,
se desploma en la tierra.

ODE TO THE BOOK (II)

We
the poets
the wanderers
we explore
the world,
in every doorway
life received us,
we engage
in the daily struggle.
What is our victory?
A book,
a book filled
with human touches,
with shirts,
a book
without solitude, with people
and tools in it,
a book
is our victory.
It lives and falls
like other fruits,
more than mere light,
more than mere shadow,
it expires,
it flutters downward,
it scatters
through the streets,
it plummets to the earth.

A student of both Neruda's and Lorca's at that time, Gabriel Celaya recalled the differences in the poetry and style of the two men—who spent part of almost every day together—by the way they commented on his poetry. Lorca would always refer to the "intention" of Celaya's poems, to their composition and structure. But Neruda would cover the margins around Celaya's poems with miniscule handwriting, aways remarking on the specific choice of words. Instead of concerning himself with the overall design, he was preoccupied with the smallest units of the poem—the individual sounds taking precedence over the grand construction of the work.

By February 1936, the Popular Front, a coalition of leftists and reformists, had gained the upper hand throughout Spain. Many social programs were implemented, including an extensive land reform to help the peasants, who in many regions still lived in a state of bondage to the landowners. These measures provoked a violent reaction from the Right. On July 17, military uprisings

Federico García Lorca, considered by many to be Spain's greatest poet, was murdered by political rightists in 1936. A grieving Neruda wrote of his friend: "I have never seen grace and genius, a winged heart and a crystalline waterfall, come together in anyone else as they did in him."

occurred throughout Spain and Morocco (then a Spanish colony), under the direction of General Emilio Mola and other conspirators, including General Francisco Franco. After a full-scale civil war broke out, the publication of *Caballo verde* was suspended. The poets of Spain now had more pressing concerns.

For Neruda, the war began on the night of July 19. In a spirit of fun, he had agreed to meet Lorca at the Circo Price Arena in order to see his first professional wrestling match. The spirit of fun quickly faded when Lorca failed to show up. Neruda went home and spent the night worrying about his friend. He later learned that Lorca had gone into hiding in the countryside near Granada. Some deep-seated impulse had driven him to go south to his native Andalusia, which was quickly falling under the control of the rightists, instead of remaining safely in Madrid. On August 16, Lorca was arrested. Two days later, he was shot along with three other men suspected of being leftists. With the murder of his friend, whom he called "the most loved, the most cherished, of all Spanish poets," Neruda became more deeply involved than ever in the fight to save the Republic.

Volunteers from all over the world were gathering to fight against the right-wing insurgents (who later became known as the Nationalists). But the insurgents—with the support of trained German and Italian soldiers who had been sent by the Fascist leaders Adolf Hitler and Benito Mussolini—were proving stronger with each month. General Francisco Franco, who was viewed by the conservatives as the savior of Spain, was appointed head of the Nationalist forces in late September 1936.

In addition to the military threat from the Right, internal feuds sapped the strength of the Republican cause. In Catalonia, one of the primary strongholds of the Republicans, the anarchist POUM (Workers Party of Marxist Unification) was ousted from the government at the Communists' insistence. (The Communists and anarchists were bitterly opposed to one another; whereas the Communists wished to create a workers' government on the model of the Soviet Union, the anarchists, who scorned all governments,

believed that the Soviet state was just another form of oppression.)
Before long, the POUM's leader, Andrés Nin, was killed by Soviet
agents after he refused to endorse their claims that his party was
controlled by the Nazis. The Spanish Communists, supported by
the Soviet Union, also withheld weapons from Republican military
units that were controlled by anarchists. As a result, important
strategic points fell to the Nationalists.

In November 1936, the Nationalists began a siege of Madrid.
They were so confident of victory that they even encouraged tour-
ism in the areas they had conquered in the north, and they publicly
vowed that Madrid would be theirs by July 1, 1938. Neruda expressed his personal defiance in a series of poems, later published
as *España en el corazón* (Spain in the Heart). These poems marked a
distinct shift in his career. Whereas his earlier work had been filled
with a mood of isolation and anguish, the new poems were, as he
put it, "stained with passion." The new tone is vividly present in
"Explico algunas cosas" (I Explain a Few Things):

> Generals
> traitors:
> look at my house void of life,
> look at Spain, broken:
> but from every dying house burning metal flows
> instead of flowers . . .
> and from every dead child a rifle with eyes,
> and from every crime bullets
> that will one day
> find you—in the heart.

España en el corazón was printed under the direction of the poet
Manuel Altolaguirre. The printing was done in a monastery on the
eastern front by soldiers who had just learned to set type. Because
there was a shortage of paper, the pages were manufactured from
any kind of cloth the soldiers could get their hands on, including a
Fascist flag and a bloody shirt taken from a Moroccan prisoner.

Benito Mussolini, Italy's Fascist leader, joined with the German dictator Adolf Hitler to support the Nationalists in Spain. With Italian and German troops and planes aiding their cause, the Nationalists were able to overthrow the Spanish Republic after three years of savage fighting.

According to Neruda, the Republican troops cherished the copies that were distributed, sometimes leaving behind food so that they could keep the books in the knapsacks. But as the Nationalist bombs fell relentlessly and the Republican troops fell back, Neruda's poems were gradually scattered to the wind. As Neruda recalled: "The last copies of this impassioned book that was born and perished in the midst of fierce fighting were immolated in a bonfire." Only a few copies of *España en el corazón* survived the war; Neruda later came across one of them on display in the Library of Congress, in Washington, D.C.

Because of his open support of the Republic, Neruda was dismissed from his consular post in Madrid. He then moved to Valencia in the east, where the Republican government had also moved as a result of the threat to Madrid. After spending a short time in Valencia, Neruda went to Paris in 1937 to help organize international support for the Republic. During that year, his wife decided that their marriage had come to an end and went back to the Netherlands with the couple's daughter.

Upon arriving in Paris, Neruda took an apartment with his friend Rafael Alberti and Alberti's wife, María Teresa León. In his book *Comiendo en Hungría* (Eating in Hungary), Neruda recalled his daily walks wih Alberti along the river Seine. On their way out, the two portly poets always stopped in front of a bookstore window to measure their waistlines against a display of the complete works of the French novelist Victor Hugo. Alberti would sadly exclaim, "Good Heavens! I have already outgrown Volume V of *Les Misérables*!" And Neruda, after measuring his own bulk against the long row of books, would reply, "I haven't put on weight. My paunch juts out only as far as *Notre-Dame de Paris.*"

Neruda went on an involuntary diet when he moved from Alberti's apartment to a small, run-down hotel with Delia del Carril, whom he had quickly married after his divorce from Maruca. The couple lived on very little money, rarely enjoying a substantial meal. Neruda spent much of his time with the French poet Paul Éluard, later confessing that if "poets answered public-opinion polls truthfully, they would give the secret away: there is nothing as beautiful as wasting time. . . . With Paul, I would lose all sense of the passing of day or night. . . . I always left Éluard's home smiling without even knowing why."

Even though Neruda was at this time walking around with holes in his shoes, he managed to organize the International Writers Congress, which met in Madrid in July 1937. The meeting was designed to rally support for the Spanish Republic, which was largely abandoned by the democratic governments of western Europe and North America. (Although these governments were opposed to fascism, they disliked Communism even more and did not want the Soviet Union to gain influence in Spain.) Among the writers who attended the conference were Ernest Hemingway, Stephen Spender, Ilya Ehrenburg, André Malraux, and Octavio Paz.

In the final analysis, the support of writers and artists was no substitute for planes, tanks, and rifles. The Republicans fought valiantly over the next two years, but by 1939, the better-armed Nationalists were victorious. A million Spaniards had been killed in the war, and a million more streamed eastward into France, seeking refuge from the victorious Nationalists. They had reason to be afraid. General Franco, installed as Spain's new head of state, became a brutal dictator. In the first year of his regime, an estimated 150,000 to 200,000 suspected leftists were killed. Franco was to rule Spain with an iron fist until his death in 1975.

Neruda returned to Chile in October 1937. His father was gravely ill. Although he was semiconscious most of the time, the old railroad man managed to express his disappointment with his son, asking Neruda one night, "Why are you so twisted? . . . Straighten yourself out." On the night of his father's death, Neruda closed himself in the study of his father's house and began to write "Almagro," his first poem about the history of Chile. His experience in Spain had reaffirmed his desire to write a different brand of poetry, one that embraced history and political struggles. "I had already done enough tramping over the irrational and the negative," he later recalled. "I had to pause and find the road to humanism, outlawed from contemporary literature but deeply rooted in the aspirations of mankind."

Neruda began to work on his *Canto general* (General Song), a long cycle of poems dealing with Latin American reality. When he found a publisher to subsidize the work, he used the money he received to buy a house on Isla Negra, a wild stretch of seacoast where he would have enough privacy to throw himself into his work. At the same time, Neruda traveled throughout the country chairing conferences and reading his poetry. In an interview in the journal *Ercilla*, he explained his political views at the time: "I am not a Communist. Nor a Socialist. Nor anything. I am simply a writer. A free writer who loves freedom. . . . I belong to the people because I

Defeated Republican troops, some of the 1 million Spaniards exiled by the civil war, show their defiant spirit in a French internment camp in 1939. Neruda called his successful effort to find a home in Chile for thousands of Spanish exiles "the crowning point of my life."

am one of them. That is why I am antifascist. My adhesion to the people is not tainted with orthodoxy nor submission."

In 1939, Neruda was appointed to another consular post, this time in Paris. There he was given the responsibility of aiding the migration of the defeated Spanish Republicans from France to Chile. The government of Chile, now controlled by a coalition of liberals and leftists, fully supported this project. But the old-line diplomats in the Chilean embassy in Paris were a conservative group, and they did everything possible to frustrate Neruda's work. Despite many obstacles, Neruda helped book the passage of 2,000 refugees aboard the *Winnipeg*, a ship purchased by the Spanish Republicans. In later years, he considered this achievement "the crowning point of my life." In his poem "El fuego cruel" (Cruel

Fire), written more than 20 years later, Neruda expressed his agony in watching the thousands of war-weary refugees retreat from Spain:

> What could we have done with innocence and anger
> when before our eyes the abundance of the world
> was spilling out
> and now death
> takes over
> table,
> bed,
> marketplace,
> theater,
> the house next door,
> and marches in armor from Albacete and Soria,
> by coast and plain, by city and river,
> street by street,
> and here it is,
> and we have only our skin to fight it with,
> only our flags and our fists,
> and our sorrowing, bleeding honor,
> with our feet broken
> on the dust and stones
> of the hard roads of Catalonia,
> marching
> under the final bullets
> into exile, oh my brave brothers!

The French author Albert Camus wrote about the effects of the Spanish civil war on his generation: "It was in Spain that men learned that one can be right and yet be beaten, that force can vanquish spirit, that there are times when outrage is not its own recompense. It is this, doubtless, which explains why so many men, the world over, feel the Spanish drama is a personal tragedy." For Neruda the war certainly was a personal tragedy, but it also increased his resolve to see the causes he believed in triumph in the Americas.

Pablo Neruda strolls through a street on the Mediterranean island of Capri in February 1952. Although the Italian government was trying to expel him for being a Communist, Neruda spent several happy months on Capri with his new love, Matilde Urrutia.

CHAPTER SIX

Discovering America

Shortly after Neruda got the Spanish refugees on board the *Winnipeg*, the German army invaded Poland. France and Great Britain declared war on Germany, and World War II was under way. "From my window in Paris," Neruda recalled, "I looked out on Les Invalides and I saw the first contingents [of French troops] leaving, youngsters who had not yet learned to wear their soldier's uniforms but were marching straight into death's gaping mouth." There was nothing more for Neruda to do in Europe. In August 1940, Chile's progressive government, appreciative of his work with the Spanish refugees, appointed Neruda consul general in Mexico. He gladly turned his attention to the New World.

In Mexico City, Neruda met the great Mexican painters Diego Rivera, José Clemente Orozco, and David Alfaro Siqueiros. At that time, these painters were best known for their murals depicting the history of Latin America and the struggle of the masses for social justice. As Neruda put it, the painters were "covering the city with history and geography, with civil strife, with fierce controversies."

The passion they brought to their work strengthened Neruda's belief that the struggle for social justice, though defeated in Spain, could succeed in Latin America.

Perhaps inspired by the colossal energy of Rivera, Neruda embarked upon a period of intense poetic creation. In his poetry, he began to take on a new role—that of spokesman for Latin America. In "Un canto para Bolívar" (A Song for Bolívar), Neruda reveals his new aspirations in an imaginary dialogue with the 19th-century Latin American liberator Simón Bolívar:

> I came upon Bolívar, one long morning,
> in Madrid, at the entrance to the Fifth Regiment.
> Father, I said to him, are you, or are you not, or who are
>   you?
> And, looking at the Mountain Barracks, he said:
> "I awake every hundred years when the people awake."

In the three years he lived in Mexico, Neruda used Mexico City as a base from which to explore the nearby regions, focusing his attention on the huge markets he found in every town. He later wrote, with an eye for color and form that was worthy of his painter friends: "Mexico is a land of crimson and phosphorescent turquoise shawls. Mexico is a land of earthen bowls and pitchers, and fruit lying open to a swarm of insects. Mexico is an infinite countryside of steel-blue century plants with yellow thorns."

Mexico was also at times a country racked by political conflict. In 1941, during a visit to Cuernavaca, Neruda and his friends were attacked by a group of pro-Nazi Germans, and Neruda was taken to the hospital with a five-inch cut on the top of his head. Although Mexico joined the alliance against fascism when the United States entered the war in 1941, Neruda was unhappy with the basic policies of Mexico's leaders. Twenty years of radical reforms had followed the Mexican revolution of 1910, but during the 1940s, Mexico was becoming more prosperous and more conservative. For Neruda, the last straw came during a strike by factory workers.

Neruda recovers from a head wound he suffered when attacked by a group of pro-Nazi Germans in Cuernavaca, Mexico, in 1942. At the time, World War II was entering its decisive phase; Neruda urged Latin Americans to join the war effort against fascism.

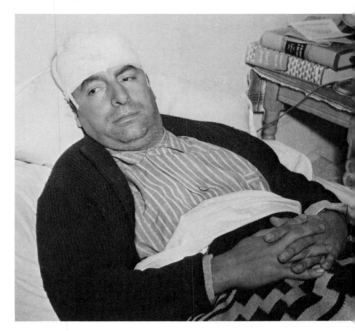

When a group of strikers' wives tried to approach the presidential palace to ask for help from the government, soldiers shot down the women in cold blood. Neruda expected a tidal wave of protest to sweep the nation; he was deeply outraged when the incident was all but ignored by the newspapers, labor leaders, and politicians. By 1943, Neruda was ready to return home.

The public acclaim he received in Panama and Bolivia and his stirring visit to Machu Picchu confirmed Neruda's commitment to political reform in Latin America. Back in Chile, he actively campaigned for the Popular Front coalition, which backed President Juan Antonio Ríos in his drive for social reform. However, when congressional elections placed the left-wing parties in control of the legislature, Ríos, afraid of losing the support of the moderates in the coalition, refused to cooperate with the parties of the political left. Foreign policy was also a source of conflict. The moderate elements in Chile did not want to take sides in World War II, which was now turning in favor of the Allies—the United States, Great Britain, and the Soviet Union. But the parties of the Left were pressing for an alliance with the Soviet Union, then waging a desperate struggle with the invading German armies. As the war continued, Neruda's own sympathies moved increasingly toward the political Left.

By the end of World War II, Neruda was a dedicated revolutionary. No longer "simply a writer," he successfully ran for the Senate and formally joined the Communist party in 1945. At this time the Communists and the Socialists were vying for the support of Chile's workers, who had become increasingly militant. Neruda did not spell out his reasons for choosing the Communist party, but he appears to have felt that he had to take a stand one way or the other. He believed that in Latin America, where there was such a huge gulf between the rich and the poor, there was little chance of gradual reform. The Communists impressed him as being the most disciplined of all the left-wing parties. In addition, the apparent success of Communism in the Soviet Union and the Soviets' crucial role in smashing the powerful German army during World War II certainly added to the party's appeal. Addressing the organization in "A mi partido" (To My Party), in *Canto general,* Neruda also expressed the personal strength he had derived from his commitment:

> You have given me the strength of all those living.
> You have restored my country to me, as though in a new
>   birth. . . .
> You have made me see the clarity of the world and the
>   possibility of joy.
> You have made me indestructible, for with you I no longer
>   end in myself.

But tolerance for Communists was not widespread in Chile, and the right-wing military was still strongly opposed to the party. When

Tenochtitlán, *a mural by the Mexican painter Diego Rivera celebrating the Aztec capital that later became Mexico City. Neruda was inspired by Rivera and other Mexican artists to write poetry that confronted the history and political reality of Latin America.*

Neruda visited the potassium nitrate mines in Chile, intending to address the workers and the union leaders, he was refused entrance into the union hall. Not to be denied, Neruda brought his listeners out to the vast desert that contained Chile's mineral wealth. In the midst of his speech, a roar was heard coming from the town. Thundering down the road, an army tank drove up to the crowd of 200 people gathered around the poet. The tank stopped about 15 feet away from Neruda, and from the turret the muzzle of a machine gun zeroed in on him. The poet refused to back down, continuing to speak even as an officer emerged from the tank and glared at him. Neruda finished his talk and, with an outward calmness that masked a justified fear, left the scene. The officer never made a move.

In 1946, Neruda was decorated with the Order of the Aztec Eagle by the Mexican government. He also became the national campaign manager for Gabriel González Videla, who was running for president of Chile. González Videla promised to help the workers and peasants, but after winning the election in a landslide, he turned on his leftist supporters. His government claimed to be reformist but actually benefited the upper and middle classes. With the backing of the United States and Chilean business interests, González Videla invested large sums in new industries but did little to help the urban and rural workers. When his former supporters began to protest, González Videla ordered the repression and detention of all Communists.

On the first evening of the crackdown, he invited some union leaders to dine with him. At the end of the evening, with tears in his eyes, González Videla told his guests: "I am weeping because I've ordered your detention. You'll be arrested as you go out the door, and I don't know if I'll ever see you again."

In October 1947, González Videla ordered a strict censorship of the Chilean press. After a month, Neruda defied the president and published an open letter, "Carta íntima para miliones de hombres" (Intimate Letter for Millions of People), in the journal *El Nacional* in Caracas, Venezuela. Neruda's article was a vigorous attack on González Videla and his policies. (Thirty years later, Neruda still detested González Videla, remembering him as a "vile, bloodthirsty vampire" and a "contemptible creature" who had "an insignificant but twisted mind.") When the president read what his former campaign manager had written about him, he initiated legal proceedings against Neruda.

At first, Neruda attempted to flee the country. But even though he had the Mexican ambassador in his car with him, the police at the border refused to let him leave. On January 6, 1948, Neruda responded by making a passionate attack on González Videla before the Chilean Senate. As a result, the Supreme Court accused

Neruda of being a Communist agitator, and on February 3, it officially banned him from the Senate.

Two days after banning him from the Senate, the Supreme Court issued an order for Neruda's arrest. The poet promptly went into hiding. With the help of the secretary general of the Communist party, Ricardo Fonseca, Neruda was moved from house to house, from city to city, for a year and a half. As he later recalled, "I passed through fields, ports, cities, camps, and was in the homes of peasants, engineers, lawyers, seamen, doctors, miners." Although he was constantly on the move, living in fear that the police or neighbors might become aware of his presence, Neruda still found time to complete *Canto general.*

At one point, Neruda's supporters proposed to smuggle him out of the country on a banana boat bound for Ecuador, but the plan fell through. As an alternative, Neruda's friends decided to take him south, where he could cross into Argentina through the mountains and be sheltered by Argentine Communists. Donning a fake beard and glasses, and with the entire manuscript of *Canto general* in hand, the poet left Santiago in the backseat of a car,

Chilean miners send a load of copper ore to the surface. After Neruda joined the Communist party in 1945, he devoted much of his energy to organizing the copper miners, who lived in poverty in the vast northern deserts that contained Chile's great mineral resources.

wrapped in blankets to augment his disguise. At noon, the car reached Temuco, Neruda's hometown. Neruda and his companions drove right through but stopped out in the countryside to have lunch. As Neruda wrote in his *Memoirs*: "There was a creek far down the slope, and the sound of its waters came up to me. It was my childhood saying goodbye."

After a long, tense stay in a lumber camp, Neruda crossed the Andes in February 1949, following a tortuous trail formerly used by smugglers. By that time he no longer needed the fake beard he had used as a disguise; his own had come in full and thick, so much so that his old friend Victor Bianchi, who had helped him get his first consular appointment, hardly recognized Neruda when he came to join the group that was leading him to safety. The group, led by expert pathfinders, set out through forests so dense that the travelers could not see the sky through the treetops. "There were no tracks, no trails; my four mounted companions and I wove in and out, overcoming such obstacles as powerful trees, impassable rivers, enormous crags, desolate snows, guessing more often than not, looking for the road to my freedom."

When the group finally arrived in San Martín de los Andes in Argentina, Neruda wrote on the wall of a cabin, "Goodbye, my country. I am leaving, but I take you with me." However, being out of Chile did not mean that he was out of danger. Notified by the Chilean government of Neruda's escape, the Argentine police were diligently searching for Neruda. He realized that he had to leave Latin America altogether, but he had no passport. The solution he came up with may be unique in the annals of literature. It happened that Neruda and Miguel Angel Asturias, the renowned Guatemalan novelist, bore a definite resemblance to one another. Asturias was, like Neruda, a diplomat and was on a mission to Buenos Aires when he was informed of Neruda's predicament. Asturias immediately agreed to lend Neruda his passport, and in this way Neruda was able to reach Paris in safety.

Once in Paris, Neruda had a new problem. He had to return Asturias's passport, reveal his true identity to the police, and admit that he had entered France illegally. It was not the sort of thing the strict French authorities were likely to appreciate. Friends advised Neruda to check into the swanky George V Hotel, where no one would trouble him about his papers, and sit tight. The strategy worked, because in a few days Neruda's cause was taken up by Pablo Picasso, the great Spanish painter who had been living in Paris since the 1920s. Picasso, a fervent leftist, used his enormous prestige as an artist and his extensive influence with the French government to secure a haven for Neruda. Through the help of a friend in the Chilean government, Neruda even got his own passport renewed, whereupon someone in the Chilean embassy in Paris insisted that the French police take it away. In Neruda's presence, the French chief of police phoned the ambassador. After a lengthy conversation, the chief said to Neruda, "He seems to be your determined enemy. But you can stay in France as long as you wish." Neruda's relief was mixed with anger because the same ambassador had just that morning sent him a friendly message.

With his papers now in order, Neruda was able to travel and did so with enthusiasm for the next three years. In 1949, he was invited to the Soviet Union to help celebrate the 150th anniversary of the birth of the Russian poet Aleksandr Pushkin. Neruda had become an international figure as a result of his persecution by the Chilean government, and in June the Union of Soviet Writers staged a tribute in his honor. Neruda was making his first visit to the world's foremost Communist nation. He was deeply impressed by the vast size of the Soviet Union and by the energy with which the Soviets were rebuilding their country after the devastation of World War II. From the standpoint of the 1990s, when Soviet-style Communism fell into disfavor throughout eastern Europe, Neruda's enthusiasm for the one-party state may seem naive or misguided. During the late 1940s, however, he was only one among many people through-

Gabriel González Videla, described by Neruda as a "bloodthirsty vampire," served as president of Chile from 1946 to 1952. When Neruda spoke out against González Videla's abuse of power, the president ordered his arrest: Neruda was forced to flee the country and live abroad for three years.

out the world who saw the Soviet Union as the champion of society's underdogs.

After visiting Poland and Hungary, Neruda traveled to Mexico with his friend Paul Éluard in August 1949. Here, however, Neruda was afflicted with a severe case of phlebitis, an inflammation of the veins, in one of his legs; suffering intense pain, he was immobilized for several months. The following year, with Neruda feeling healthy once again, the first complete edition of *Canto general* was printed in Mexico. It was a huge collection of poetry, representing almost a decade's work, including the remarkable "Alturas de Macchu Picchu." The first edition, comprising 15 volumes and 568 pages, was accompanied by the illustrations of the Mexican painters David Alfaro Siqueiros and Diego Rivera. Included in *Canto general* were bitter accounts of the torture and abuse suffered by Chileans under President González Videla. As a result, Neruda's book was banned in Chile, appearing only in an underground edition. In addition to attacking Latin American dictators, Neruda also skewered North American business interests. In "La United Fruit Co.," he condemns with heavy sarcasm the economic domination of the United States over Latin America:

When the trumpet sounded,
everything was prepared on earth
and Jehovah divided the world
among Coca Cola Inc., Anaconda,
Ford Motors, and other corporations.
For the United Fruit Company Inc.
the juiciest was reserved,
the central coast of my land,
the sweet waist of America.

While still in Mexico, Neruda met Matilde Urrutia, the woman
who would later inspire his greatest love poetry. A Chilean from the
rural south, Urrutia would travel with Neruda to India, China, and
Italy during the next two years. From this time they spent together,
especially some months on the Mediterranean island of Capri,
Neruda's next work emerged—*Los versos del capitán* (The Captain's
Verses). When the book was published anonymously in Naples,
Italy, in 1952, several critics suggested that Neruda had left his
name off the book to avoid displeasing the Communist party:
Rather than dealing with political issues, the book celebrated the
daily pains and pleasures of love. But Neruda later insisted that he
had concealed his authorship to avoid hurting Delia del Carril, to
whom he was still legally married. "This book, filled with sudden
and burning love, would have reached her like a rock hurled
against her gentleness." Neruda and Carril had spent 18 years
together, but for the rest of Neruda's life Urrutia would be his
constant companion.

While traveling through northern Europe, Neruda received
good news from Chile. González Videla had been replaced by the
man called the General of Hope, Carlos Ibañez del Campo. Although Neruda would later have his disagreements with Ibañez del
Campo as well, the new president revoked the orders for Neruda's
arrest. In 1952, more than three years after going into exile, the
poet was free to return home.

Pablo Neruda, photographed during the 1950s. At this time, Neruda was at the height of his fame. He was a popular hero in Chile, and his poems had been translated into languages as diverse as Russian, Arabic, and Japanese.

CHAPTER SEVEN

Poet of the People

In August 1952, Neruda arrived in Santiago as a conquering hero. At this point, his poetry had been translated into numerous languages, including Russian, Polish, Hebrew, Korean, Vietnamese, Japanese, Hungarian, and Arabic. Neruda had truly become an international figure, identified not only with left-wing political causes but also, because of his persecution by the Chilean government, with the principle of free expression. Even those writers who disagreed with Neruda's political views admired his poetry and his refusal to be muzzled by politicians and the police.

In 1954, writers from around the world arrived in Santiago to help celebrate Neruda's 50th birthday. The participants included Ilya Ehrenburg from the Soviet Union, Ai Ch'ing from China, Miguel Angel Asturias from Guatemala, and María Rosa Oliver from Argentina. To mark the occasion, Neruda decided to give a present—a very large one—to the University of Chile. Along with 5,000 books he had collected throughout his travels, he donated a large number of manuscripts and valuable first editions. As part of his donation, Neruda gave his entire shell collection to the university as well. (Later, Neruda would bitterly regret his generosity when he learned that all his books and precious shells had disappeared, apparently through mismanagement and neglect.)

In 1955, Neruda painfully separated from Delia del Carril, his wife of 18 years. Shortly afterward, he moved into his new house in Santiago with Matilde Urrutia, whom he later married. This was to be the last upheaval in Neruda's often tumultuous personal life. In his book *Cien sonetos de amor* (One Hundred Love Sonnets), Neruda revealed to Urrutia how she fulfilled his emotional needs:

> Everything was empty, dead, and silent,
> fallen, abandoned, and decayed:
> everything was inalienably foreign to me,
> everything belonged to others and to no one:
> until your beauty and your poverty
> filled the autumn with gifts.

Neruda was no longer the starving poet who had walked the streets of Paris with holes in his shoes. Royalties from the sale of his books and cash awards connected to literary prizes now made it possible for him to leave the diplomatic service and enjoy life. Neruda established three residences in Chile during the 1950s, and together they expressed his personality and imagination almost as much as his poetry did. First, there was the oceanfront house he had bought in 1939 in Isla Negra, overlooking the Pacific, where he and Urrutia were able to relax and take long walks along the beach. (Isla Negra, which means "black island," is in actuality not an island at all but rather a small fishing village located about 25 miles south of Valparaíso, distinguished by winding dirt paths and huge pine trees.) La Chascona, Neruda's house on Marqués de la Plata Street in Santiago, was right next to the zoo and provided a splendid view of the city. The most unusual of the three houses was La Sebastiana in Valparaíso, the great seaport that had enchanted Neruda during his student days. La Sebastiana, built next to a movie theater,

La Chascona, Neruda's house in Santiago, was one of three homes he established in Chile during the 1950s. La Chascona was right next to the city's zoo, which Neruda always loved to visit, and provided a splendid view of the city from its hilltop setting.

featured huge windows that provided spectacular views of the city and the harbor.

These three homes were barely enough to shelter the vast array of objects that Neruda had accumulated during years of haunting junkyards and antique shops around the world. He had collections of butterflies, moths, and ships in bottles, in addition to the 15,000 seashells he donated to the University of Chile. In one of his offices there was a large wooden horse, and a small locomotive—no doubt a tribute to his father—sat in the garden of one of his houses. But the most dramatic objects in his collections were his figureheads. These large carved figures, usually of women, had once graced the bows of sailing ships but now peered out from the corners and stairways of Neruda's homes, startling visitors with their lifelike presence. In *Memoirs*, Neruda confessed the pleasure he took in his cherished objects: "The child who doesn't play is not a child, but the man who doesn't play has lost forever the child who lived in him, and he will certainly miss him. I have also built my house like a toy house, and I play in it from morning till night."

Perhaps inspired by the time he spent decorating his houses, Neruda was beginning a new period of poetic development. In his book *Odas elementales* (Elemental Odes), he added the simple pleasure he took in everyday things to the wide array of his usual subjects. Originally written for the Caracas newspaper *El Nacional* in weekly installments, his alphabetically ordered odes ranged in subject from "Oda al aire" (Ode to the Air) to "Oda al vino" (Ode to Wine), stopping along the way to celebrate the Americas, hope, the fertility of the earth, the Soviet city of Leningrad, books, numbers, autumn, poverty, and the tomato. *Odas elementales* was first published in Buenos Aires and received wide critical acclaim.

Writing and collecting did not interfere with Neruda's impulse to travel. In 1952, he made a grand tour of various Communist countries, including China. After he received the Stalin Peace Prize the following year, he and Urrutia made annual trips to Europe so that he could serve as a jurist for the prize. Throughout these years, he never strayed from his public support of the Communist party, even after he learned of the brutal purges conducted in the Soviet Union during the 1930s and 1940s under the orders of Premier Joseph Stalin. During the purges, millions of innocent people accused by Stalin of disloyalty to the Soviet state were either executed by the secret police or sent to prison camps, where they died of overwork and starvation. These horrors were revealed and denounced by Soviet leader Nikita Khrushchev during the Twentieth Party Congress in 1956. At that time, many Communists and Communist sympathizers turned away from the party in disillusion and disgust. Neruda was among those who remained faithful, choosing to regard Stalin's crimes as unfortunate mistakes rather than fundamental defects of Communist rule. It was not until late in his life, in his last collections of poems and memoirs, that Neruda would admit that in his fervent support of the Soviet revolution he had been "blind to the sinister details."

Neruda's apparently unshakable loyalty to the Communist party continued to cause him trouble in Latin America. In 1957,

Soviet premier Nikita Khrushchev addresses a massive rally in Budapest, Hungary, in 1958. Two years earlier, Khrushchev had stunned the world by exposing atrocities committed by the regime of Joseph Stalin during the 1930s and 1940s. Despite this news, Neruda maintained his faith in the Soviet system.

Neruda was invited to the Congress for Peace in Colombo, Ceylon. Eager to revisit the places he had lived in as a young man, Neruda accepted the invitation. On his way to Ceylon, however, Neruda stopped in Argentina to give some poetry readings. On the night of April 11, the Argentine secret police burst into the house where he and Urrutia were staying and went through all his luggage. Upon learning that Neruda was confined to bed by another attack of phlebitis, the police went away and came back an hour later with an ambulance. They had orders to take Neruda to jail, no matter what, and they proceeded to shift him onto a stretcher. The policemen carrying the stretcher had a terrible time getting Neruda's bulk down the stairs, but they followed their orders and locked him in a cell, where he was greeted with affection by many of the prisoners. Within hours, the Chilean consulate and several Argentine writers demanded Neruda's release, and he was freed the following day. As he was leaving the jail, one of the guards quickly thrust a poem into his hand. Dedicated to Neruda, it had been written by the guard himself that very night. "I imagine few poets have received a poetic homage from the men assigned to guard them," Neruda reflected.

Although Neruda later asserted that nothing remarkable happened to him during the 1950s, these years marked the pinnacle of his career as a public figure. Neruda himself was not shy about claiming that the downtrodden masses of Latin America spoke through his poetry, and this opinion was shared by many people throughout the world. Wherever Neruda and Urrutia went, large crowds formed to hear the poet read his work. Audiences were mesmerized by his deep, gravelly voice and his commanding presence at the podium. Returning often to Eastern Europe and the Soviet Union, where he was always welcomed because of his loyalty to the Communist party, Neruda was showered with honors, receptions, and thunderous applause.

Apparently, Neruda's popularity extended even to the animal kingdom. On one of his trips to the Soviet Union, he made a visit to Yerevan, the capital of Armenia, and indulged in one of his great passions, visiting the zoo. While there he came across a tapir, a docile South American animal related to the rhinoceros. Neruda had a special affection for tapirs; he admitted that their heavy bodies, long noses, and small eyes made them look very much like a certain well-known Chilean poet. Recalling the meeting with his fellow Latin American, Neruda was sure that the tapir also saw the resemblance: "When he saw me his eyes lit up. . . . They opened a small door for him. He threw me a happy look and plunged into the water, puffing like some fabled sea horse, like a hairy triton." After the tapir had finished his acrobatic performance, the zoo-keeper told Neruda, "We've never seen him so happy."

Despite his international reputation, Neruda did not allow himself to become complacent as a writer. Beginning in 1958 with *Estravagario* and throughout the 1960s, he was extremely prolific, producing 8 collections of new poetry in 10 years. In this later poetry, Neruda was turning from the world of everyday objects and political struggles and exploring the more private and somber regions of his life. *Cien sonetos de amor*, his most frankly emotional poetry, was completed soon after *Estravagario*. In the introduction to the sonnets (poems of 14 lines each that usually follow a strict rhyming pattern), Neruda wrote to Urrutia:

Walking in forests or on beaches, along hidden lakes, in latitudes sprinkled with ashes, you and I have picked up pieces of pure bark, pieces of wood subject to the comings and goings of water and the weather. Out of such softened relics, then, with hatchet and machete and pocketknife, I built up these lumber piles of love, and with fourteen boards each I built little houses, so that your eyes, which I adore and sing to, might live in them.

In 1961, the one-millionth copy of *Veinte poemas de amor* was printed, and rumors began to spread about the possibility of Neruda's receiving the Nobel Prize for literature. He and Urrutia stocked up on provisions and padlocked the gate to their home in Isla Negra as if preparing for a siege. Beyond the gate, reporters from around the world were poised to swoop in and interview the prospective Nobel Prize winner. But after a few days of suspense, the Swedish Academy in Stockholm awarded the prize to the Greek poet George Seferis. Neruda unlocked his garden gate. The reporters had vanished.

In 1966, Neruda embarked on his first reading tour of the United States. He was invited by the PEN Club, an international

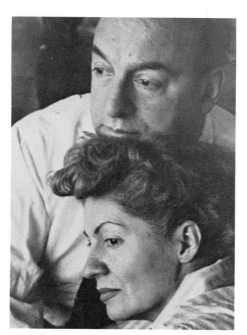

Neruda with Matilde Urrutia, who became his constant companion after he separated from his second wife, Delia del Carril. Although Neruda continued to write on political themes, Urrutia inspired one of his most popular books, Cien sonetos de amor *(One Hundred Love Sonnets).*

writers' organization that champions the right of free expression. It came as no surprise to anyone when the U.S. State Department objected to Neruda's visit and refused to grant him an entry visa. Ever since the end of World War II, anti-Communism had been a powerful force in the political life of the United States, and foreign citizens who had any kind of Communist affiliation were usually barred from entering the country, even for only a short visit. In Neruda's case, the PEN Club lodged a vigorous protest with the State Department. Prominent American writers, such as Arthur Miller and Marianne Moore, defended Neruda's right to read his poetry and the public's right to hear him. The government relented, and Neruda made his first visit to the United States.

At his first reading in New York, such a large crowd gathered to hear the controversial poet that closed-circuit cameras had to be set up in order for the people gathered outside the auditorium to see him. From New York, Neruda moved on to Washington, D.C., and Berkeley, California; in both of those cities he made tapes of his poetry readings on behalf of the Library of Congress. During his trip, Neruda was moved by the way people responded to his poetry and his ideas. He may have been somewhat naive in concluding that many North Americans shared his political views, but the visit was from any standpoint a great success.

Heading south from California, Neruda gave a number of readings in Mexico City and then visited Peru for the first time in 20 years. It was not necessary for him to revisit Machu Picchu; his great poem had, as he discovered, "become a part of Peruvian life." When he received a decoration from the Peruvian president Fernando Belaúnde, he considered the honor as more than a merely personal tribute. He was well aware that throughout their history, the nations of Chile and Peru had feuded over borders and mineral rights, sometimes engaging in full-scale military action. Neruda had always maintained close friendships with Peruvian writers and saw his decoration as part of a larger healing process: "Not only athletes, diplomats, and statesmen must take pains to stanch that blood from the past, but poets also, and with all the more reason, for their souls have fewer frontiers than the souls of other people."

Despite the success of his visit to North America, the unavoidable conflict between the sensitive poet and the public figure was finding expression in Neruda's poetry at this time. In his collection *Las manos del día* (The Hands of the Day), there is an unsettling sense of guilt. For the first time, Neruda begins to publicly question his party's decisions. He was especially troubled by the Soviet Union's 1968 invasion of Czechoslovakia, undertaken to suppress that country's move toward independence from Soviet domination. The first crack in his happy relations with the party had come two years earlier, when a group of Cuban writers published a letter accusing him of knuckling under to the U.S. government during his 1966 visit. Neruda, who had supported Cuba's Communist revolution since its beginning in 1958, was outraged by this charge. Although the Chilean Communist party made a point of giving Neruda a medal of their own on his return, the attitude of the Cubans had a lasting and painful impact on him.

Even his admirers were beginning to irritate Neruda. In "Abejas (I)" (Bees), Neruda addressed the journalists and critics who were constantly hounding him about his life and work:

> They follow me, inquiring
> into my relations with cats,
> how I discovered the rainbow,
> why the noble chestnut trees
> put forth their burrs;
> above all they want to know
> what the bullfrogs think of me,
> and the animals concealed
> beneath the fragrant forests
> or in pimples of cement.

Although the bullfrogs remained silent, the Swedish Academy soon expressed its opinion.

Neruda speaks with reporters after winning the 1971 Nobel Prize for literature. In his acceptance speech, Neruda asserted his belief that writers should involve themselves wholeheartedly in the political struggles of the people.

CHAPTER EIGHT

Triumph and Sorrow

Before he had any thought of receiving the Nobel Prize, Neruda enjoyed a distinction only a handful of writers have ever known: He ran for the presidency of his country. Although Neruda had no desire to be president of Chile, the Communist party wanted a strong and visible candidate for the 1970 election, and party leaders visited Isla Negra to make a personal plea for Neruda's services. He accepted the nomination, but only on the condition that he could pull out whenever he wanted to. He also knew that the chances of a Communist winning the election were very slim. He fully expected that the party would eventually enter a coalition to back a different candidate from the Left.

As he traveled about the country making speeches and meeting the people, Neruda's enthusiasm for the election began to mount. Despite his humble background and his sympathy for the working class, Neruda had actually spent most of his time with writers and artists. The daily give-and-take with ordinary people on the campaign trail was a new experience for him, and he made the most of it. He even began to wonder what he would do if he were actually elected president of a nation whose political and economic problems had never been solved.

Neruda was greatly relieved when the moderate socialist Salvador Allende emerged as the candidate of the Popular Unity party, a coalition of left-wing groups that included the Communists. All the Popular Unity groups, despite their differences, agreed on a basic program—to improve the lot of the workers and distribute land to the peasants. To Neruda and many Chileans, Allende appeared to be the ideal man to achieve these ends. He had helped found the Chilean Socialist party in 1933 and had served in the Senate from 1945 to 1969. He was also a seasoned campaigner, having already run for the presidency three times. With the Popular Unity coalition firmly in place and many Chileans ready for a change, it looked as though Allende's moment had finally arrived.

Having gladly resigned his own candidacy, Neruda devoted himself to campaigning for Allende. He was amazed by the stamina Allende displayed during long campaign trips through the seemingly endless length of Chile. Allende had the knack of falling asleep in the car during the drives between towns and villages. When the car stopped, Allende would be wide awake: He would

Neruda campaigning during the 1970 Chilean presidential election. Neruda agreed to be the candidate of the Communist party only because he felt he had no chance of winning. However, he discovered that he enjoyed going out among the people and even began to think he might like to be president.

jump out, greet the people, and make a speech. As soon as he was back in the car, he would fall asleep again. No matter how hectic the schedule was, his energy never waned.

Allende's tireless campaigning paid off. In the election, held on September 4, 1970, he received 36.3 percent of the general vote, more than any other candidate. But because he failed to achieve a majority, it was up to the Congress to choose the new president. Usually, the Congress chose whoever got the most votes. But in this case, another factor was at work.

U.S. president Richard Nixon, convinced that Allende would do great harm to U.S. business interests in Chile, wanted desperately to prevent Allende from becoming the leader of Chile. The U.S. Central Intelligence Agency (CIA) had spent $425,000 during the election to distribute anti-Allende literature, but this had proved to be ineffective. President Nixon and his chief adviser, Secretary of State Henry Kissinger, quickly developed a plan to prevent Allende from taking office. Concealing their activities from the public, Nixon and Kissinger tried to persuade the Chilean military to take over the government; at the same time, they worked to sabotage Allende's election in Congress by pressuring and bribing individual members.

The Nixon-Kissinger plan failed. Although there were members of the Chilean military who would have supported a coup, General René Schneider, the commander in chief of the Chilean armed forces, vowed to support the Congress in its choice for president. At the same time, any large-scale attempt to influence the Chilean Congress was judged by the CIA to be too risky. Allende was elected president by a vote of 153–35 in the Congress and was inaugurated on November 3, 1970. "For one hundred and eighty years," Neruda wrote, "the same kind of rulers under different labels had succeeded one another in my country, and they all did the same thing. The rags, the disgraceful housing, the children without schools or shoes, the prisons, and the cudgeling of my poor people continued. . . . Now we could breathe and sing."

Salvador Allende waves to his supporters in October 1970, after learning that he had been elected president of Chile. Neruda had thrown his support to Allende during the campaign; with Allende leading the nation, he believed, Chileans would be able to "breathe and sing."

Neruda's pleasure in Allende's election was mixed with serious concerns for his own health. At the age of 66, he was suffering from cancer. Despite Neruda's medical problems, President Allende appointed the poet ambassador to France a few weeks after taking office. In Chile, as in the United States, ambassadors had to be approved by the Senate, and Neruda just barely scraped by with three votes more than necessary. (Of the senators who had publicly praised his poetry but feared his political views, Neruda wrote, "Of course it's obvious that they would have much preferred making these speeches at my funeral.")

Neruda arrived in Paris in March 1971 in a buoyant spirit. "I was pleased at the idea of representing a victorious popular government," he recalled, "after so many years of mediocre and lying ones." He had not forgotten the abuse he had been subjected to by his fellow diplomats in 1939 when he was struggling to find refuge for the Spanish exiles. He took a measure of revenge by removing the portraits of all the former ambassadors from the walls of the embassy and replacing them with portraits of his own Chilean heroes, including Allende and Luis Emilio Recabarren, the founder of the Chilean Communist party. The rest of the embassy staff—conservative civil servants who retained their jobs despite changes in the government—immediately began to worry about their new boss.

Almost as soon as Neruda arrived in Paris, rumors began to swirl that he was finally going to receive the Nobel Prize for literature. With the results of the election about to be announced, journalists invaded the Chilean embassy on the morning of October 21, 1971. Neruda had received a message from the Swedish ambassador requesting an interview in the afternoon; but he had no indication that it was about the prize, so he refused to make any statements to the press. The tension in the lobby was building as the frustrated journalists began to lose patience with Neruda's evasiveness. Finally, a Parisian radio station broke the news: Neruda had won the prize. Although he was still weak after a recent operation, Neruda managed to get through the unavoidable news conference as well as an evening of celebration with friends from Europe and Latin America.

When he accepted the prize in Stockholm, Neruda pointedly expressed his views on the connection between literature and politics: "In the midst of the arena of America's struggles I saw that my human task was none other than to join the extensive forces of the organized masses of the people, to join with life and soul, with suffering and hope, but it is only from this great popular stream that the necessary changes can arise for writers and for nations." He concluded his speech with a message of hope: "Lastly, I wish to say to the people of good will, to the workers, to the poets, that the whole future has been expressed in this line by Rimbaud: 'Only with a *burning patience* can we conquer the splendid City, which will give light, justice, and dignity to all mankind.'"

In November 1972, Neruda left his post in Paris and returned to Chile. Although some biographers have claimed that he went home because of his failing health, Matilde Urrutia was quick to point out that Neruda's main reason for returning was his realization that many people in Chile were anxious to congratulate him on his Nobel Prize. In addition, he was eager to see the ocean from his southern home again.

Neruda's first public appearance in Chile was at the National Stadium of Santiago, where Neruda read his latest poetry to an enthusiastic throng. However much he relished the adulation of his fellow Chileans, the fact remained that Neruda was now slowly dying of cancer; the two operations he had undergone in Europe had left him in a weakened state. He was not cheered by some of the things he began to see on the streets of Santiago, especially the posters and acts of violence directed against the Left. The atmosphere reminded him of the pro-Nazi ferment he had witnessed in Paris on the eve of World War II.

During his first two years in office, Allende had instituted a number of reforms. Major industries had been nationalized, or taken over by the government, which planned to channel the profits into programs that would benefit the workers. Allende's government increased the minimum wage, provided free milk for children and food programs for working mothers, and improved medical care for the poor. In the countryside, three-fourths of Chile's large estates had been broken up in order to provide land to the peasants.

U.S. president Richard Nixon (left) and his secretary of state, Henry Kissinger, conferring in the White House. Nixon and Kissinger were convinced that Allende's reforms would harm U.S. business interests in Chile, so they developed a secret plan to destroy his government.

But Allende had also made powerful enemies both within Chile and abroad. Anaconda and Kennecott, the giant U.S. copper companies, were outraged by the price Allende offered them for their holdings in Chile. Along with other U.S. firms, they urged the Nixon administration to get tough with the Chileans. The administration needed little urging. On orders from Nixon and Kissinger, the CIA stepped up its support of right-wing groups, and the U.S. government began an economic blockade of Chile. Because of this blockade, Chile could not get parts for any U.S.-made motor vehicles or industrial equipment. As the economy began to suffer, the government slowly lost support, especially among the growing middle class. If this group joined the conservative interests that had opposed Allende from the start, the government was headed for a major crisis.

Neruda and many others believed that the United States was the crucial factor in Allende's eventual downfall. In the introduction to *Incitación al Nixonicidio y alabanza de la revolución chilena* (A Call for the Destruction of Nixon and Praise for the Chilean Revolution), Neruda declared that he would make "no excuses: Against the enemies of my people my song is offensive and hard as Araucanian stone. . . . Steady, now I'm going to fire."

In the midst of Chile's turmoil and his desperate battle with cancer, Neruda found a haven in his remote and peaceful home in Isla Negra. This peace was disturbed occasionally by the loud whir of helicopter blades: Whenever he could get away, President Allende would come to Isla Negra unannounced to visit his friend. At Isla Negra, Neruda seemed to come closer than ever to realizing one of his dreams, "to remain forever, before the fire, near the sea, with two dogs, reading the books it was so hard to collect, smoking my pipes."

In her book *Mi vida junto a Pablo Neruda* (My Life with Pablo Neruda), Urrutia remembered that September 11, 1973, started off like any other day at Isla Negra. The writer Fernando Alegría was expected for lunch, and Neruda was happy, looking forward to something he always loved to receive—a recently printed book. A new edition of his book *Canción de gesta* (Song of Protest) was to arrive that day, the culmination of months of work by the poet.

Neruda and Urrutia did not suspect that Chile was at that moment on the edge of a political earthquake. When he turned on the radio to listen to the news, Neruda looked at Urrutia in shock— he heard the voice of Salvador Allende, declaring that he was at La Moneda and would resist to the end. Early that morning, the military had launched a CIA-backed coup designed to oust Allende and crush his supporters. This was the last time that Neruda and Urrutia would hear their friend's voice.

On other stations, a military junta (council) was proclaiming itself the government of Chile, ordering all citizens to report the names of anyone engaged in leftist activities to the police. Many of the country's moderate forces supported the coup in the belief that the military dictatorship would be a brief transitional phase. They hoped that Chile would soon return to how it had been before 1970. After the military announced Operation Silence, which was implemented to cut off all opposing broadcasts, those stations that did not forthrightly support the junta quickly faded into static.

In Santiago, La Moneda was quickly encircled by military forces under the direction of General Augusto Pinochet. Allende's first concern was the safety of the women in the palace, who included a number of staff members and two of his granddaughters. At first he pleaded with them to leave, but after they refused, claiming they wanted to stay by his side, he gruffly ordered the women out of the palace, escorting them personally to a side door. The newspaper reporter Frida Modak, Allende's press secretary, remembered that the president then picked up the intercom to the guardhouse outside the palace and said to the commanding general: "There is a group of women who are going to leave La Moneda. And even though you are a traitor, General, I would expect that you will at least have the decency to give these young women safe conduct and provide them with a jeep to get them out of the area of combat."

After two minutes of silence, the general agreed to take the women out. At 11:00 A.M., the military began a full-scale assault on La Moneda. By early afternoon, Allende was dead and his government destroyed.

Though it is not clear whether Allende took his own life rather than face inevitable defeat or was shot by Pinochet's men, Neruda remained among the many who believed that Allende was assassinated. To them it seems unlikely that one who had donned a steel helmet and armed himself with a machine gun minutes before his death, and who had refused to surrender despite the recommendations of his immediate aides, would have taken his own life. Others argue that Allende simply committed suicide rather than surrender. The issue is not important, however, as there is little doubt that regardless of who pulled the trigger, it was Nixon, Kissinger, the CIA, and Pinochet who in 1973 brought about the death, and possibly the murder, of the freely elected president of Chile.

Within hours of Allende's death, all democratic institutions ceased to exist in Chile. The Congress was suspended, and strikes were declared illegal. The military used tanks to bombard working-class neighborhoods where Allende supporters lived. Fires broke

With the backing of the United States, General Augusto Pinochet (center) led a 1973 military coup that toppled the Allende government and touched off a reign of terror in Chile. Pinochet's triumph was a bitter blow to Neruda, who was slowly dying of cancer.

out. Resistance fighters struck back, but their small arms were no match for the might of Pinochet's forces. Many Allende supporters were rounded up and either jailed, placed in concentration camps, or exiled. When the jails began to overflow, alleged dissidents were herded into soccer stadiums, where they were held captive. More than 10,000 people were taken prisoner by Pinochet's henchmen within a month of Allende's death. While most of the international community condemned Pinochet's actions, refused to recognize the junta, and broke off diplomatic relations with Chile, the United States officially recognized Pinochet's government shortly after Allende's demise.

The leading generals of the junta tightened their grip on the press and also tried to suppress the words of Neruda and other left-wing writers. Within the week, soldiers arrived at Neruda's house in Isla Negra. Carrying machine guns and bazookas, one detachment took up positions around Neruda's property; another burst through the front door and began to search the house. Neruda could put up no resistance. Suffering great pain, he had been able to do nothing but lie in bed and watch television coverage of the coup's progress. When the soldiers had gone, Urrutia decided that Neruda needed to be in a hospital, and she called for an ambulance.

On the way to Santiago, the ambulance was repeatedly stopped and searched at roadblocks set up by the military. Urrutia tried to protest, pointing out that Neruda was seriously ill, but each time, the troops insisted on a thorough search before allowing the ambulance to pass. After one stop, when Urrutia was ordered out of the ambulance so that the soldiers could be sure there was nothing illegal inside, she returned to find Neruda with tears in his eyes. She knew that he was not crying for himself or even for her. The poet's tears had fallen for Chile.

A few days later, La Chascona, Neruda's home in Santiago, was also ransacked. Vandals started a bonfire in the garden and burned the poet's vast and highly treasured book collection. Torn-up books and manuscripts were scattered throughout the house. A pipe had been smashed on the second floor, soaking everything with water. Neruda's house in Valparaíso soon suffered the same fate.

Grief stricken by Allende's death and the triumph of the Right, Neruda languished in the hospital. He was powerless to help his friends, many of whom were being rounded up by soldiers and herded into Santiago's National Stadium. Many were never seen again. Although he had every reason to despair, Neruda clung to his hope for a better future. For several days, the dying poet drifted between semiconsciousness and spurts of energy, during which he tried to read and even to dictate the last paragraphs of his autobiography.

On September 23, 1973, Pablo Neruda died of a heart attack in his hospital bed. Although La Chascona was a shambles, Urrutia decided to hold the wake there, anyway. Friends and neighbors helped her get Neruda's body into the house, building a makeshift bridge across the canal that ran in front of the property. On the day

Chilean women mourn at Neruda's funeral in September 1973. Despite the danger of arrest, a large crowd filled the streets around Neruda's house in Santiago and followed his coffin to the cemetery.

of the funeral, the neighboring streets were filled with people. Everyone was carefully dressed because casual clothing was looked on with suspicion by Chile's new rulers, who considered jeans and long hair a sure sign of leftist tendencies. Defying the authorities, who had threatened mass arrests, members of the crowd began to yell, "Neruda, we salute you!" Upon reaching the cemetery, the crowd boldly broke into the Communist anthem "The Internationale."

After the funeral, Urrutia returned to La Chascona alone. Stepping across the threshold, she felt a cold, damp breeze blowing through the broken doors and windows. Folding her arms, she braced herself against the cold, struggling to remember the good times La Chascona had seen. Speaking some time later at a memorial for Neruda, she said: "It was joy that Pablo loved; and for that reason, I'm not going to ask here that we remember him with a minute's silence. No—I'm going to ask for Pablo a minute of joy—a lot of noise, much applause."

Following his death, Neruda's homes were ransacked by the authorities and declared off limits to the public. However, the poet's admirers defiantly continued to visit the properties: The fence outside the house at Isla Negra was soon covered with tributes to Neruda and quotations from his poetry.

Although Neruda's memory would be officially repressed under General Pinochet's brutal regime, for years to come his admirers—among them many couples who had been inspired by his love poems—secretly went to Isla Negra to carve messages in the fence posts surrounding his home. So many words were inscribed on the fence that the Colombian novelist Gabriel García Márquez wrote: "If anybody had the patience to do it, the complete poems of Pablo Neruda could be reconstructed from the scattered verses written from memory on the fence boards by lovers." One tribute in particular echoes the faith in humanity that Neruda never lost:

> Generals: Love never dies
> Pablo we want to love as you loved
> One minute of darkness will not make us blind.

Chronology

July 12, 1904	Born Neftalí Ricardo Reyes Basoalto in Parral, Chile; mother dies one month later
1906	Father remarries and moves to Temuco with Neftalí
1919	Thirteen poems by Neftalí published in *Corre-Vuela*
1920	Neftalí adopts pseudonym Pablo Neruda
1921	Moves to Santiago to study at Instituto Pedagógico
1924	*Veinte poemas de amor y una canción desesperada* is published
1927	Neruda appointed consul in Rangoon, Burma; for the next five years, serves at various consulates in Asia
1930	Marries María Antonieta Hagenaar Vogelzanz
1932	Returns to Santiago, which is in midst of economic depression
1933	Appointed to a consular post in Buenos Aires, Argentina
1934	Serves as a consul in Barcelona, Spain; daughter Malva Marina is born

1936	Outbreak of Spanish civil war; Federico García Lorca murdered by rightists
1937	Neruda and María Antonieta Hagenaar Vogelzanz separate; Neruda marries Argentine painter Delia del Carril
1940	Named consul general in Mexico
1945	Elected to Chilean Senate; joins the Communist party; writes "Alturas de Macchu Picchu"
1947	Denounces Chilean government; President González Videla initiates political action against him
1948	Neruda declared a Communist agitator by Chilean Supreme Court; goes into hiding after arrest is ordered
1949	Flees Chile; travels throughout Europe
1950	*Canto general* published in Mexico
1952	Chilean government declares amnesty for Neruda, and he returns to Chile
1955	Neruda separates from Delia del Carril; moves in with Matilde Urrutia
1957	Arrested in Buenos Aires; Chilean consul obtains his release two days later
1964	*Memorial de Isla Negra* published in five volumes
1966	Neruda travels to United States as guest of PEN Club

1970	After briefly running for presidency of Chile, supports campaign of Salvador Allende; Allende elected president; Neruda appointed ambassador to France
1971	Receives Nobel Prize for literature
1972	Returns to Chile
Sept. 11, 1973	Popular Unity government overthrown; Allende dies of gunshot wounds; reign of terror begins in Chile
Sept. 23, 1973	Neruda dies in a hospital in Santiago

Further Reading

Agostin, Marjorie. *Pablo Neruda*. Boston: Twayne, 1986.

Bizzarro, Salvatore. *Pablo Neruda: All Poets the Poet*. Metuchen, NJ: Scarecrow, 1979.

Bloom, Harold, ed. *Pablo Neruda*. New York: Chelsea House, 1989.

Chavkin, Samuel. *The Murder of Chile*. New York: Everest House, 1982.

De Costa, René. *The Poetry of Pablo Neruda*. Cambridge: Harvard University Press, 1979.

Durán, Manuel, and Margery Safir. *Earth Tones: The Poetry of Pablo Neruda*. Bloomington: Indiana University Press, 1981.

Felstiner, John. *Translating Neruda: The Way to Macchu Picchu*. Stanford: Stanford University Press, 1980.

Gilbert, Rita. *Seven Voices*. New York: Knopf, 1973.

Mitchell, David. *The Spanish Civil War*. New York: Watts, 1983.

Neruda, Pablo. *Canto General.* Translated by Jack Schmitt. Berkeley: University of California Press, 1991.

———. *The Captain's Verses.* Translated by Donald D. Walsh. New York: New Directions, 1972.

———. *Five Decades: Poems, 1925–1970.* Translated by Ben Bellitt. New York: Grove Press, 1974.

———. *The Heights of Macchu Picchu.* Translated by Nathaniel Tarn. New York: Farrar, Straus & Giroux, 1967.

———. *Isla Negra: A Notebook.* Translated by Alastair Reid. New York: Farrar, Straus & Giroux, 1981.

———. *Memoirs.* Translated by St. Martin Hardie. New York: Penguin Books, 1978.

———. *One Hundred Love Sonnets.* Translated by Stephen Tapscott. Austin: University of Texas Press, 1986.

———. *Passions and Impressions.* Translated by Margaret S. Peden. New York: Farrar, Straus & Giroux, 1983.

———. *Residence on Earth.* Translated by Donald D. Walsh. New York: New Directions, 1973.

———. *Selected Poems: A Bilingual Edition.* Boston: Houghton Mifflin, 1970.

————. *Twenty Love Poems and a Song of Despair.* New York: Norton, 1990.

Poirot, Luis. *Pablo Neruda: Absence and Presence.* New York: Norton, 1990.

Santi, Enrico M. *Pablo Neruda: The Politics of Prophecy.* Ithaca, NY: Cornell University Press, 1982.

Zubatsky, David S., and Hensley C. Woodbridge. *Pablo Neruda: An Annotated Bibliography.* New York: Garland, 1986.

Index

JOSEPH ROMAN is a freelance writer currently residing in New York. The recipient of a George Peabody Gardner Traveling Fellowship, he has studied and traveled extensively in Latin America.

RODOLFO CARDONA is professor of Spanish and comparative literature at Boston University. A renowned scholar, he has written many works of criticism, including *Ramón, a Study of Gómez de la Serna and His Works* and *Visión del esperpento: Teoría y práctica del esperpento en Valle-Inclán*. Born in San José, Costa Rica, he earned his B.A. and M.A. from Louisiana State University and received a Ph.D. from the University of Washington. He has taught at Case Western Reserve University, the University of Pittsburgh, the University of Texas at Austin, the University of New Mexico, and Harvard University.

JAMES COCKCROFT is currently a visiting professor of Latin American and Caribbean studies at the State University of New York at Albany. A three-time Fulbright scholar, he earned a Ph.D. from Stanford University and has taught at the University of Massachusetts, the University of Vermont, and the University of Connecticut. He is the author or coauthor of numerous books on Latin American subjects, including *Neighbors in Turmoil: Latin America, The Hispanic Experience in the United States: Contemporary Issues and Perspectives*, and *Outlaws in the Promised Land: Mexican Immigrant Workers and America's Future*.